THE NATIONAL ACADEMIES
Advisers to the Nation on Science, Engineering, and Medicine

The **National Academy of Sciences** is a private, nonprofit, self-perpetuating society of distinguished scholars engaged in scientific and engineering research, dedicated to the furtherance of science and technology and to their use for the general welfare. Upon the authority of the charter granted to it by the Congress in 1863, the Academy has a mandate that requires it to advise the federal government on scientific and technical matters. Dr. Ralph J. Cicerone is president of the National Academy of Sciences.

The **National Academy of Engineering** was established in 1964, under the charter of the National Academy of Sciences, as a parallel organization of outstanding engineers. It is autonomous in its administration and in the selection of its members, sharing with the National Academy of Sciences the responsibility for advising the federal government. The National Academy of Engineering also sponsors engineering programs aimed at meeting national needs, encourages education and research, and recognizes the superior achievements of engineers. Dr. C. D. Mote, Jr., is president of the National Academy of Engineering.

The **Institute of Medicine** was established in 1970 by the National Academy of Sciences to secure the services of eminent members of appropriate professions in the examination of policy matters pertaining to the health of the public. The Institute acts under the responsibility given to the National Academy of Sciences by its congressional charter to be an adviser to the federal government and, upon its own initiative, to identify issues of medical care, research, and education. Dr. Victor J. Dzau is president of the Institute of Medicine.

The **National Research Council** was organized by the National Academy of Sciences in 1916 to associate the broad community of science and technology with the Academy's purposes of furthering knowledge and advising the federal government. Functioning in accordance with general policies determined by the Academy, the Council has become the principal operating agency of both the National Academy of Sciences and the National Academy of Engineering in providing services to the government, the public, and the scientific and engineering communities. The Council is administered jointly by both Academies and the Institute of Medicine. Dr. Ralph J. Cicerone and Dr. C. D. Mote, Jr., are chair and vice chair, respectively, of the National Research Council.

www.national-academies.org

Identifying the Culprit

Assessing Eyewitness Identification

Committee on Scientific Approaches to Understanding and Maximizing
the Validity and Reliability of Eyewitness Identification
in Law Enforcement and the Courts

Committee on Science, Technology, and Law

Policy and Global Affairs

Committee on Law and Justice

Division of Behavioral and Social Sciences and Education

NATIONAL RESEARCH COUNCIL
OF THE NATIONAL ACADEMIES

THE NATIONAL ACADEMIES PRESS
Washington, D.C.

THE NATIONAL ACADEMIES PRESS   500 Fifth Street, NW   Washington, DC 20001

NOTICE: The project that is the subject of this report was approved by the Governing Board of the National Research Council, whose members are drawn from the councils of the National Academy of Sciences, the National Academy of Engineering, and the Institute of Medicine. The members of the committee responsible for the report were chosen for their special competences and with regard for appropriate balance.

This study was funded by a grant between the National Academy of Sciences and the Laura and John Arnold Foundation. Any opinions, findings, conclusions, or recommendations expressed in this publication are those of the author and do not necessarily reflect the views of the organization that provided support for the project.

International Standard Book Number13:   978-0-309-31059-8
International Standard Book Number10:   0-309-31059-8
Library of Congress Control Number: 2014955458

Additional copies of this report are available from the National Academies Press, 500 Fifth Street, NW, Room 360, Washington, DC 20001; (800) 624-6242 or (202) 334-3313; http://www.nap.edu.

Staff

ANNE-MARIE MAZZA, Study Director and Director, Committee on Science, Technology, and Law

ARLENE F. LEE, Director, Committee on Law and Justice

STEVEN KENDALL, Program Officer, Committee on Science, Technology, and Law

KAROLINA KONARZEWSKA, Program Coordinator, Committee on Science, Technology, and Law

ANJALI SHASTRI, Christine Mirzayan Science and Technology Policy Graduate Fellow

SARAH WYNN, Christine Mirzayan Science and Technology Policy Graduate Fellow

COMMITTEE ON SCIENCE, TECHNOLOGY, AND LAW

Co-Chairs

DAVID BALTIMORE (NAS/IOM), President Emeritus and Robert Andrews Millikan Professor of Biology, California Institute of Technology

DAVID S. TATEL, Judge, U.S. Court of Appeals for the District of Columbia Circuit

Members

THOMAS D. ALBRIGHT (NAS), Professor and Director, Vision Center Laboratory and Conrad T. Prebys Chair in Vision Research, Salk Institute for Biological Studies

ANN ARVIN (IOM), Lucile Packard Professor of Pediatrics and Microbiology and Immunology; Vice Provost and Dean of Research, Stanford University

BARBARA E. BIERER, Professor of Medicine, Harvard Medical School

CLAUDE CANIZARES (NAS), Vice President and the Bruno Rossi Professor of Physics, Massachusetts Institute of Technology

ARTURO CASADEVALL (IOM), Leo and Julia Forchheimer Professor of Microbiology and Immunology; Chair, Department of Biology and Immunology; and Professor of Medicine, Albert Einstein College of Medicine

JOE S. CECIL, Project Director, Program on Scientific and Technical Evidence, Division of Research, Federal Judicial Center

R. ALTA CHARO (IOM), Warren P. Knowles Professor of Law and Bioethics, University of Wisconsin at Madison

HARRY T. EDWARDS, Judge, U.S. Court of Appeals for the District of Columbia Circuit

DREW ENDY, Associate Professor, Bioengineering, Stanford University and President, The BioBricks Foundation

MARCUS FELDMAN (NAS), Burnet C. and Mildred Wohlford Professor of Biological Sciences, Stanford University

JEREMY FOGEL, Director, Federal Judicial Center

HENRY T. GREELY, Deane F. and Kate Edelman Johnson Professor of Law and Professor, by courtesy, of Genetics, Stanford University

MICHAEL GREENBERGER, Law School Professor and Director, Center for Health and Homeland Security, University of Maryland

BENJAMIN W. HEINEMAN, JR., Senior Fellow, Harvard Law School and Harvard Kennedy School of Government

DAVID WEISBURD, Distinguished Professor, Department of Criminology, Law and Society and Director, Center for Evidence-Based Crime Policy, George Mason University; Walter E. Meyer Professor of Law and Criminal Justice, The Hebrew University Faculty of Law

CATHY SPATZ WIDOM, Distinguished Professor, Psychology Department, John Jay College of Criminal Justice, The City University of New York

PAUL K. WORMELI, Executive Director, Integrated Justice Information Systems

Staff

ARLENE F. LEE, Director
EMILY BACKES, Research Associate
MALAY MAJMUNDAR, Senior Program Officer
STEVE REDBURN, Scholar
JULIE SCHUCK, Senior Program Associate
DANIEL TALMAGE, Program Officer
TINA M. LATIMER, Program Coordinator

Acknowledgments

ACKNOWLEDGMENT OF PRESENTERS

The committee gratefully acknowledges the contributions of the following individuals:

Karen L. Amendola, *Police Foundation*; Steven E. Clark, *University of California, Riverside*; Rob Davis, *Police Executive Research Forum*; Kenneth Deffenbacher, *University of Nebraska at Omaha*; Paul DeMuniz, *Oregon Supreme Court*; Shari Seidman Diamond, *Northwestern University and American Bar Foundation*; John Firman, *International Association of Chiefs of Police*; Ronald Fisher, *Florida International University*; Geoffrey Gaulkin, *Special Master, State v. Henderson (NJ)*; Kristine Hamann, *National District Attorney's Association*; Barbara Hervey, *Texas Court of Criminal Appeals*; Robert J. Kane, *Supreme Judicial Study Group on Eyewitness Identification (MA)*; Saul Kassin, *John Jay College of Criminal Justice*; Peter Kilmartin, *State of Rhode Island*; David LaBahn, *Association of Prosecuting Attorneys*; Elizabeth F. Loftus, *University of California, Irvine*; Roy S. Malpass, *University of Texas at El Paso*; Sheri Mecklenburg, *U.S. Department of Justice*; Christian A. Meissner, *Iowa State University*; John Monahan, *University of Virginia*; Steven D. Penrod, *John Jay College of Criminal Justice*; P. Jonathon Phillips, *National Institute of Standards and Technology*; Joseph Salemme, *Chicago Police Department*; Daniel L. Schacter, *Harvard University*; Barry Scheck, *The Innocence Project*; Jessica Snowden, *Federal Judicial Center*; Nancy K. Steblay, *Augsburg College*; Gary L. Wells, *Iowa State University*; John T. Wixted, *University of California, San Diego*; David V. Yokum, *University of Arizona*.

ACKNOWLEDGMENT OF REVIEWERS

This report has been reviewed in draft form by individuals chosen for their diverse perspectives and technical expertise, in accordance with procedures approved by the National Academies' Report Review Committee. The purpose of this independent review is to provide candid and critical comments that will assist the institution in making its published report as sound as possible and to ensure that the report meets institutional standards for objectivity, evidence, and responsiveness to the study charge. The review comments and draft manuscript remain confidential to protect the integrity of the process.

We wish to thank the following individuals for their review of this report: Art Acevedo, Austin, Texas Police Department; Aaron Benjamin, University of Illinois at Urbana-Champaign; Vicki Bruce, Newcastle University; Jules Epstein, Widener University; Jeremy Fogel, Federal Judicial Center; Constantine Gatsonis, Brown University; Henry T. Greely, Stanford University; Peter Imrey, Cleveland Clinic; Robert Kane, Massachusetts Supreme Court; Timothy Koller; Office of the Richmond County District Attorney; Elizabeth Loftus, University of California, Irvine; Robert Masters, Office of the Queens County District Attorney; Geoffrey Mearns, Northern Kentucky University; and Hal Stern, University of California, Irvine.

Although the reviewers listed above have provided many constructive comments and suggestions, they were not asked to endorse the conclusions or recommendations, nor did they see the final draft of the report before its release. The review of this report was overseen by David Korn, Harvard Medical School and Massachusetts General Hospital and Stephen E. Fienberg, Carnegie Mellon University. Appointed by the National Academies, they were responsible for making certain that an independent examination of this report was carried out in accordance with institutional procedures and that all review comments were carefully considered. Responsibility for the final content of this report rests entirely with the authoring committee and the institution.

Preface

Eyewitness identifications play an important role in the investigation and prosecution of crimes, but they have also led to erroneous convictions. In the fall of 2013, the Laura and John Arnold Foundation called upon the National Academy of Sciences (NAS) to assess the state of research on eyewitness identification and, when appropriate, make recommendations. In response to this request, the NAS appointed an ad hoc study committee that we have been privileged to co-chair.

The committee's review analyzed relevant published and unpublished research, external submissions, and presentations made by various experts and interested parties. The research examined fell into two general categories: (1) basic research on vision and memory and (2) applied research directed at the specific problem of eyewitness identification.

Basic research has progressed for many decades, is of high quality, and is largely definitive. Research of this category identifies principled and insurmountable limits of vision and memory that inevitably affect eyewitness accounts, bear on conclusions regarding accuracy, and provide a broad foundation for the committee's recommendations.

Through its review, the committee came to recognize that applied eyewitness identification research has identified key variables affecting the accuracy of eyewitness identifications. This research has been instrumental in informing law enforcement, the bar, and the judiciary of the frailties of eyewitness identification testimony. Such past research has appropriately identified the variables that may affect an individual's ability to make an accurate identification. However, given the complex nature of eyewitness identification, the practical difficulties it poses for experimental research, and the still ongoing evolution of statistical procedures in the field of eyewitness identification research, there remains at the time of this review substantial uncertainty about the effect and the interplay of these variables on eyewitness identification. Nonetheless, a range of practices has been validated by scientific methods and research and represents a starting place for efforts to improve eyewitness identification procedures.

In this report, the committee offers recommendations on how law enforcement and the courts may increase the accuracy and utility of eyewitness identifications. In addition, the committee identifies areas for future research and for collaboration between the scientific and law enforcement communities.

We are indebted to those who addressed the committee and to those who submitted materials to the committee, and we are particularly indebted to the members of the committee. These individuals devoted untold hours to the review of materials, meetings, conference calls, analyses, and report writing. This report is very much the result of the enormous contributions of an engaged community of scholars and practitioners who reached their findings and recommendations after many vigorous and thoughtful discussions. We also would like to thank the project staff, Karolina Konarzewska, Steven Kendall, Arlene Lee, and Anne-Marie Mazza, and editor Susanna Carey for their dedication to the project and to the work of the committee.

Thomas D. Albright and Jed S. Rakoff
Committee Co-chairs

Contents

BOXES, FIGURES, AND TABLES

Boxes

Figures

Tables

Summary

E yewitnesses play an important role in criminal cases when they can identify culprits.[1] Yet it is well known that eyewitnesses make mistakes and that their memories can be affected by various factors including the very law enforcement procedures designed to test their memories. For several decades, scientists have conducted research on the factors that affect the accuracy of eyewitness identification procedures. Basic research on the processes that underlie human visual perception and memory have given us an increasingly clear picture of how eyewitness identifications are made and, more important, an improved understanding of the principled limits on vision and memory that may lead to failures of identification. Basic research has been complemented by a growing body of applied research on eyewitness identification, which has examined those variables that particularly affect eyewitnesses to crimes: *system variables* (conditions such as the procedures followed to obtain identifications that can be controlled by law enforcement) and *estimator variables* (conditions associated with the actual crime, such as viewing conditions, or factors specific to the eyewitness, such as the race of the victim relative to that of the perpetrator, that cannot be controlled by law enforcement).

Through such scientific research, we have learned that many factors influence the visual perceptual experience: dim illumination and brief viewing times, large viewing distances, duress, elevated emotions, and the presence of a visually distracting element such as a gun or a knife. Gaps in sensory

---

[1]Throughout this report, the term *identification* denotes person recognition. *Eyewitness identification* refers to recognition by a witness to a crime of a culprit unknown to the witness.

input are filled by expectations that are based on prior experiences with the world. Prior experiences are capable of biasing the visual perceptual experience and reinforcing an individual's conception of what was seen. We also have learned that these qualified perceptual experiences are stored by a system of memory that is highly malleable and continuously evolving, neither retaining nor divulging content in an informational vacuum. The fidelity of our memories to actual events may be compromised by many factors at all stages of processing, from encoding to storage to retrieval. Unknown to the individual, memories are forgotten, reconstructed, updated, and distorted. Therefore, caution must be exercised when utilizing eyewitness procedures and when relying on eyewitness identifications in a judicial context.

In 2013, the Laura and John Arnold Foundation called on the National Academy of Sciences (NAS) to appoint an ad hoc study committee to:

1. critically assess the existing body of scientific research as it relates to eyewitness identification;
2. identify any gaps in the existing body of literature and suggest appropriate research questions to pursue that will further our understanding of eyewitness identification and that might offer additional insight into law enforcement and courtroom practice;
3. provide an assessment of what can be learned from research fields outside of eyewitness identification;
4. offer recommendations for best practices in the handling of eyewitness identifications by law enforcement;
5. offer recommendations for developing jury instructions;
6. offer advice regarding the scope of a Phase II consideration of neuroscience research as well as any other areas of research that might have a bearing on eyewitness identification; and
7. write a consensus report with appropriate findings and recommendations.

The committee heard from numerous experts, practitioners, and stakeholders and reviewed relevant published and unpublished literature as well as submissions provided to the committee. In this report, the committee offers its findings and recommendations for:

- identifying and facilitating best practices in eyewitness procedures for the law enforcement community;
- strengthening the value of eyewitness identification evidence in court; and
- improving the scientific foundation underpinning eyewitness identification.

OVERARCHING FINDINGS

The committee is confident that the law enforcement community, while operating under considerable pressure and resource constraints, is working to improve the accuracy of eyewitness identifications. These efforts, however, have not been uniform and often fall short as a result of insufficient training, the absence of standard operating procedures, and the continuing presence of actions and statements at the crime scene and elsewhere that may intentionally or unintentionally influence eyewitness' identifications.

Basic scientific research on human visual perception and memory has provided an increasingly sophisticated understanding of how these systems work and how they place principled limits on the accuracy of eyewitness identification.[2] Basic research alone is insufficient for understanding conditions in the field, and thus has been augmented by studies applied to the specific practical problem of eyewitness identification. Applied research has identified key variables that affect the accuracy and reliability of eyewitness identifications and has been instrumental in informing law enforcement, the bar, and the judiciary of the frailties of eyewitness identification testimony.

A range of best practices has been validated by scientific methods and research and represents a starting place for efforts to improve eyewitness identification procedures. A number of law enforcement agencies have, in fact, adopted research-based best practices. This report makes actionable recommendations on, for example, the importance of adopting "blinded" eyewitness identification procedures. It further recommends that standardized and easily understood instructions be provided to eyewitnesses and calls for the careful documentation of eyewitness' confidence statements. Such improvements may be broadly implemented by law enforcement now. It is important to recognize, however, that, in certain cases, the state of scientific research on eyewitness identification is unsettled. For example, the relative superiority of competing identification procedures (i.e., simultaneous versus sequential lineups) is unresolved.

The field would benefit from collaborative research among scientists and law enforcement personnel in the identification and validation of new best practices that can improve eyewitness identification procedures. Such a foundation can be solidified through the use of more effective research designs (e.g., those that consider more than one variable at a time, and in

---

[2]Basic research on vision and memory seeks a comprehensive understanding of how these systems are organized and how they operate generally. The understanding derived from basic research includes principles that enable one to predict how a system (such as vision or memory) might behave under specific conditions (such as those associated with witnessing a crime) and to identify the conditions under which it will operate most effectively and those under which it will fail. Applied research, by contrast, empirically evaluates specific hypotheses about how a system will behave under a particular set of real-world conditions.

different study populations to ensure reproducibility and generalizability), more informative statistical measures and analyses (i.e., methods from statistical machine learning and signal detection theory to evaluate the performance of binary classification tasks), more probing analyses of research findings (such as analyses of consequences of data uncertainties), and more sophisticated systematic reviews and meta-analyses (that take account of current guidelines, including transparency and reproducibility of methods).

In view of the complexity of the effects of both system and estimator variables and their interactions on eyewitness identification accuracy, better experimental designs that incorporate selected combinations of these variables (e.g., presence or absence of a weapon, lighting conditions, etc.) will elucidate those variables with meaningful influence on eyewitness performance, which can, in turn, inform law enforcement practice of eyewitness identification procedures. To date, the eyewitness literature has evaluated procedures mostly in terms of a single diagnosticity ratio or an ROC (Receiver Operating Characteristic) curve; even if uncertainty is incorporated into the analysis, many other powerful tools for evaluating a "binary classifier" are available and worthy of consideration.[3] Finally, syntheses of eyewitness research has been limited to meta-analyses that have not been conducted in the context of systematic reviews. Systematic reviews of stronger research studies need to conform to current standards and be translated into terms that are useful for decision makers.

The committee here offers a summary of its key recommendations to strengthen the effectiveness of policies and procedures used to obtain accurate eyewitness identifications.

RECOMMENDATIONS TO ESTABLISH BEST PRACTICES FOR THE LAW ENFORCEMENT COMMUNITY

The committee's review of law enforcement practices and procedures, coupled with its consideration of the scientific literature, has identified a number of areas where eyewitness identification procedures could be strengthened. The practices and procedures considered here involve acquisition of data that reflect a witness' identification and the contextual factors that bear on that identification. A recurrent theme underlying the committee's recommendations is development of and adherence to guidelines that are consistent with scientific standards for data collection and reporting.

---

[3]T. Hastie, R. Tibshirani, and J. H. Friedman, *The Elements of Statistical Learning: Data Mining, Inference, and Prediction* (New York: Springer, 2009).

Recommendation #1: Train All Law Enforcement Officers in Eyewitness Identification

The committee **recommends** that all law enforcement agencies provide their officers and agents with training on vision and memory and the variables that affect them, on practices for minimizing contamination, and on effective eyewitness identification protocols.

Recommendation #2: Implement Double-Blind Lineup and Photo Array Procedures

The committee **recommends** blind (double-blind or blinded) administration of both photo arrays and live lineups and the adoption of clear, written policies and training on photo array and live lineup administration.

Recommendation #3: Develop and Use Standardized Witness Instructions

The committee **recommends** the development of a standard set of easily understood instructions to use when engaging a witness in an identification procedure.

Recommendation #4: Document Witness Confidence Judgments

The committee **recommends** that law enforcement document the witness' level of confidence verbatim at the time when she or he first identifies a suspect.

Recommendation #5: Videotape the Witness Identification Process

The committee **recommends** that the video recording of eyewitness identification procedures become standard practice.

RECOMMENDATIONS TO STRENGTHEN THE VALUE OF EYEWITNESS IDENTIFICATION EVIDENCE IN COURT

The best guidance for legal regulation of eyewitness identification evidence comes not from constitutional rulings, but from the careful use and understanding of scientific evidence to guide fact-finders and decision-makers. The *Manson v. Brathwaite* test under the Due Process Clause of the U.S. Constitution for assessing eyewitness identification evidence was established in 1977, before much applied research on eyewitness identification had been conducted. This test evaluates the "reliability" of eyewitness identifications using factors derived from prior rulings and not from empirically validated sources. As critics have pointed out, the *Manson v. Brathwaite* test includes factors that are not diagnostic of reliability. Moreover, the test treats factors such as the confidence of a witness as independent markers of reliability when, in fact, it is now well established that confidence judgments may vary over time and can be powerfully swayed by many factors. While some states have made minor changes to the due process framework, wholesale reconsideration of this framework is only a recent development.

Recommendation #6: Conduct Pretrial Judicial Inquiry

The committee **recommends** that, as appropriate, a judge make basic inquiries when eyewitness identification evidence is offered.

Recommendation #7: Make Juries Aware of Prior Identifications

The committee **recommends** that judges take all necessary steps to make juries aware of prior identifications, the manner and time frame in which they were conducted, and the confidence level expressed by the eyewitness at the time.

Recommendation #8: Use Scientific Framework Expert Testimony

The committee **recommends** that judges have the discretion to allow expert testimony on relevant precepts of eyewitness memory and identifications.

Recommendation #9: Use Jury Instructions as an Alternative Means to Convey Information

The committee **recommends** the use of clear and concise jury instructions as an alternative means of conveying information regarding the factors that the jury should consider.

RECOMMENDATIONS TO IMPROVE THE SCIENTIFIC FOUNDATION UNDERPINNING EYEWITNESS IDENTIFICATION RESEARCH

Basic scientific research on visual perception and memory provides important insight into the factors that can limit the fidelity of eyewitness identification. Research targeting the specific problem of eyewitness identification complements basic scientific research. However, this strong scientific foundation remains insufficient for understanding the strengths and limitations of eyewitness identification procedures in the field. Many of the applied studies on key factors that directly affect eyewitness performance in the laboratory are not readily applicable to actual practice and policy. Applied research falls short because of a lack of reliable or standardized data from the field, a failure to include a range of practitioners in the establishment of research agendas, the use of disparate research methodologies, failure to use transparent and reproducible research procedures, and inadequate reporting of research data. The task of guiding eyewitness identification research toward the goal of evidence-based policy and practice will require collaboration in the setting of research agendas and agreement on methods for acquiring, handling, and sharing data.

Recommendation #10: Establish a National Research Initiative on Eyewitness Identification

The committee **recommends** the establishment of a National Research Initiative on Eyewitness Identification.

Recommendation #11: Conduct Additional Research on System and Estimator Variables

The committee **recommends** broad use of statistical tools that can render a discriminability measure to evaluate eyewitness performance and a rigorous exploration of methods that can lead to more conservative responding. The committee further **recommends** that caution and care be used when considering changes to any existing lineup procedure, until such time as there is clear evidence for the advantages of doing so.

CONCLUSION

Eyewitness identification can be a powerful tool. As this report indicates, however, the malleable nature of human visual perception, memory, and confidence; the imperfect ability to recognize individuals; and policies governing law enforcement procedures can result in mistaken identifications with significant consequences. New law enforcement training protocols, standardized procedures for administering lineups, improvements in the handling of eyewitness identification in court, and better data collection and research on eyewitness identification can improve the accuracy of eyewitness identifications.

1

Introduction

Accurate eyewitness identifications[1] may aid in the apprehension and prosecution of the perpetrators of crimes. However, inaccurate identifications may lead to the prosecution of innocent persons while the guilty party goes free. It is therefore crucial to develop eyewitness identification procedures that achieve maximum accuracy and reliability.

Eyewitness evidence is not infallible. In 1932, Yale University law professor Edwin M. Borchard documented nearly seventy cases of miscarriage of justice caused by eyewitness errors in his book, *Convicting the Innocent*.[2] Years later, in 1967, the U.S. Supreme Court highlighted the danger of erroneous eyewitness identification in *United States v. Wade*, stating, "The vagaries of eyewitness identification are well-known; the annals of criminal law are rife with instances of mistaken identification."[3]

The Federal Bureau of Investigation (FBI) estimates that U.S. law enforcement made 12,196,959 arrests in 2012. The FBI estimates that 521,196 of these arrests were for violent crimes.[4] Accurate data on the number of crimes observed by eyewitnesses are not available. If only a fraction of the violent crimes in the United States involve an eyewitness, the number must

---

[1]Throughout this report, the term *identification* denotes person recognition. *Eyewitness identification* refers to recognition by a witness to a crime of a culprit unknown to the witness.

[2]Edwin M. Borchard, *Convicting the Innocent: Sixty-Five Actual Errors of Criminal Justice* (New York: Garden City Publishing Company, Inc., 1932).

[3]*United States v. Wade*, 388 U.S. 230, 288 (1967).

[4]Federal Bureau of Investigation, "Crime in the United States 2012: Persons Arrested," available at: http://www.fbi.gov/about-us/cjis/ucr/crime-in-the-u.s/2012/crime-in-the-u.s.-2012/persons-arrested/persons-arrested.

BOX 1-1
The Ronald Cotton Case[a]

In 1984, a college student named Jennifer Thompson was raped in her apartment in Burlington, North Carolina. The police asked her to help create a composite sketch of the rapist. The police then received a tip that a local man named Ronald Cotton resembled the composite, and shortly after the crime, Thompson was shown a photo array containing six photos. With some difficulty, she chose two pictures, one of which was of Cotton. Finally, she said, "I think this is the guy," pointing to Cotton. "You're sure," the lead detective asked, and she responded, "Positive." Thompson asked, "Did I do OK?" The detectives responded, "You did great." She has described how those encouraging remarks had the effect of making her more confident in her identification.

The police then showed Thompson a live lineup. Cotton was the only person repeated from the prior photo array. This would make Cotton more familiar and might suggest that he was the prime suspect. Nevertheless, Thompson remained hesitant and was having trouble deciding between two people. After several minutes, she told the police that Cotton "looks the most like him." The lead detective asked "if she was certain," and she said, "Yes." Again, the detectives further reinforced her decision. The lead detective told Thompson, "It's the same person you picked from the photos." She later described feeling a "huge amount of relief" when told that she had again picked the right person.

At Ronald Cotton's criminal trial, Thompson agreed she was "absolutely sure" that he was the rapist. Cotton was sentenced to life in prison plus 54 years. He served 10.5 years before DNA tests exonerated him and implicated another man, Bobby Poole. Not only did the identification procedures increase Thompson's confidence in the mistaken memory event, but they also resulted in her rejection of the actual culprit. Poole had been presented to Thompson at a post-trial hearing, and she could not recognize him. "I have never seen him in my life," she said at the time.

In response to this error, the lead detective in the case, Mike Gauldin, later as police chief, was the first in the state to institute a series of new practices, including double-blind lineup procedures. In the years that followed, North Carolina adopted such practices statewide. Ronald Cotton and Jennifer Thompson have since written a book, *Picking Cotton*, that describes their case and experiences.

---

[a]See, generally, http://www.cbsnews.com/news/eyewitness-how-accurate-is-visual-memory/ and http://www.slate.com/articles/news_and_politics/jurisprudence/features/2011/getting_it_wrong_convicting_the_innocent/how_eyewitnesses_can_send_innocents_to_jail.html.

be sizable. One estimate based on a 1989 survey of prosecutors suggests that at least 80,000 eyewitnesses make identifications of suspects in criminal investigations each year.[5]

Recently, post-conviction DNA exonerations of innocent persons have dramatically highlighted the problems with eyewitness identifications.[6,7] In the United States, more than 300 exonerations have resulted from post-conviction DNA testing since 1989.[8] According to the Innocence Project, at least one mistaken eyewitness identification was present in almost three-quarters of DNA exonerations.[9] In many of these cases, eyewitness identification played a significant evidentiary role, and almost without exception, the eyewitnesses who testified expressed complete confidence that they had chosen the perpetrator. Many eyewitnesses testified with high confidence despite earlier expressions of uncertainty.[10] For example, in the well-known case of Ronald Cotton (see Box 1-1), Jennifer Thompson (the victim) has described how she was initially quite unsure of her eyewitness identification of Cotton, a man later exonerated by DNA testing. She became certain it was Cotton only after the police made confirmatory remarks and had her participate in two identification procedures where Cotton was the only person shown both times.

Erroneous eyewitness identifications can occur across the range of criminal convictions in which eyewitness evidence is presented, but most of these cases lack the biological material that can be tested for DNA and used for exoneration purposes. While eyewitness misidentifications may have been a dominant factor in some erroneous convictions, it is important to note that other factors, including errors at various stages of the legal and judicial processes, may have contributed to the erroneous convictions.

CHARGE TO THE COMMITTEE

In 2013, the Laura and John Arnold Foundation called on the National Research Council (NRC) to assess the state of scientific research on

---

[5]A. G. Goldstein, J. E. Chance, and G. R. Schneller, "Frequency of Eyewitness Identification in Criminal Cases: A Survey of Prosecutors," *Bulletin of the Psychonomic Society* 27(1): 71, 73 (January 1989).

[6]CNN, "Exonerated: Cases by the Numbers," December 4, 2013, available at: http://www.cnn.com/2013/12/04/justice/prisoner-exonerations-facts-innocence-project/.

[7]Taryn Simon, "Freedom Row," *New York Times Magazine*, January 26, 2003.

[8]The Innocence Project, "DNA Exoneree Case Profiles," available at: http://www.innocenceproject.org/know/.

[9]The Innocence Project, "Eyewitness Identification," available at: http://www.innocenceproject.org/fix/Eyewitness-Identification.php.

[10]Brandon L. Garrett, *Convicting the Innocent: Where Criminal Prosecutions Go Wrong* 63–68 (Cambridge, MA: Harvard University Press, 2011).

BOX 1-2
Charge to the Committee

The charge to the NRC was to:

1. critically assess the existing body of scientific research as it relates to eyewitness identification;
2. identify any gaps in the existing body of literature and suggest, as appropriate, research questions to pursue that will further our understanding of eyewitness identification and that might offer additional insight into law enforcement and courtroom practice;
3. provide an assessment of what can be learned from research fields outside of eyewitness identification;
4. offer recommendations for best practices in the handling of eyewitness identifications by law enforcement;
5. offer recommendations for developing jury instructions;
6. offer advice regarding the scope of a Phase II consideration of neuroscience research as well as any other areas of research that might have a bearing on eyewitness identification; and
7. write a consensus report with appropriate findings and recommendations.

---

eyewitness identification and to recommend best practices[11] for handling eyewitness identifications by law enforcement and the courts. The goal of this effort was to evaluate the scientific basis for eyewitness identification, to help establish the scientific foundation for effective real-world practices, and to facilitate the development of policies to improve eyewitness identification validity in the context of the American justice system.

In response to this charge, the NRC appointed an ad hoc committee, the Committee on Scientific Approaches to Understanding and Maximizing the Validity and Reliability of Eyewitness Identification in Law Enforcement and the Courts (hereinafter, the committee), to undertake this study (see Box 1-2 for the committee's charge). The committee met three times, held numerous conference calls, heard from various stakeholders (see Appendix B), and reviewed extensive research on eyewitness identification before reaching its findings and recommendations.

---

[11]For the purposes of this report, the committee characterizes *best practice* as the adoption of standardized procedures based on scientific principles. The committee does not make any endorsement of practices designated as best practices by other bodies.

SCIENCE AND LAW

Law enforcement officers investigating crimes rely on eyewitness identification procedures to verify that a suspect is the individual seen by an eyewitness.[12] Such procedures can take place under conditions that may have significant effects on the accuracy and reliability of an eyewitness' identification. Unlike officers in the field, laboratory researchers have, in theory, greater control over influences that might contaminate the visual perceptual experience and memory of an eyewitness.

Science is a self-correcting enterprise. Researchers formulate and test hypotheses using observations and experiments, which are then subject to independent review. In science, evidence and data are analyzed and experiments are repeated to ensure that biases or other factors do not lead to incorrect conclusions. Scientific progress results from the review and revision of earlier results and conclusions.

The culture of scientific research is markedly different from a legal culture that must seek definitive results in individual cases. In 1993, in *Daubert v. Merrell Dow Pharmaceuticals, Inc.*, the U.S. Supreme Court ruled that, under Rule 702 of the Federal Rules of Evidence (which covers both civil and criminal trials in the federal courts), a "trial judge must ensure that any and all scientific testimony or evidence admitted is not only relevant, but reliable."[13]

Criminal justice and legal personnel have come to rely on eyewitness evidence. Law enforcement officials have first-hand experience with eyewitnesses in criminal investigations and trials, and over the years, some juridictions have implemented and strengthened practices and procedures in an attempt to improve acccuracy. Consequently, the law enforcement and legal communities have made important contributions to our understanding of eyewitness identifications and the improvements of practices in the field. Researchers have become increasingly involved in assessing eyewitness identification procedures as law enforcement, lawyers, and judges have themselves sought more accurate procedures and approaches. In the 2009 National Research Council report, *Strengthening Forensic Science in the United States: A Path Forward*, the committee noted, "in addition to protecting innocent persons from being convicted of crimes that they did not commit, we are also seeking to protect society from persons who have

---

[12]For ease of reading, throughout the report the committee will use the term *officer* to mean law enforcement officials and professionals.

[13]*Daubert v. Merrell Dow Pharmaceuticals, Inc.*, 509 U.S. 579 (1993). The Court also noted that "there are important differences between the quest for truth in the courtroom and the quest for truth in the laboratory. Scientific conclusions are subject to perpetual revision. Law, on the other hand, must resolve disputes finally and quickly."

committed criminal acts."[14] This shared common goal of protecting innocent persons and society makes collaboration between the scientific, law
enforcement, and legal communities critically important.

IDENTIFYING THE CULPRIT

Officers typically use three procedures to identify a perpetrator whose
identity is unknown: (1) showups; (2) presentations of photo arrays; and
(3) live lineups. A showup is a procedure in which officers present a single
criminal suspect to a witness. This procedure usually occurs near the crime
location and immediately or shortly after the crime has occurred. Officers
also use photo arrays and live lineups, in which they ask the witness to view
numerous individuals, one of whom may be the perpetrator. The suspect is
presented along with *fillers* (known non-suspects). Currently, photo arrays
are used more often than live lineups.[15,16]

If the eyewitness makes a positive identification during a showup, a
photo array, or a lineup, the identification may constitute evidence about a
suspect's involvement in a crime. The eyewitness identification may, when
considered with other available evidence, establish probable cause to support an arrest. Such evidence may play a pivotal role in enabling the prosecution to meet its burden of proof in a subsequent trial.

In recent years, more law enforcement agencies have created written
eyewitness identification policies and have adopted formalized training.
However, there are many agencies that do not have standard written policies or formalized training for the administration of identification procedures or for ongoing interactions with witnesses.[17]

VISION AND MEMORY

At its core, eyewitness identification relies on brain systems for visual
perception and memory: The witness perceives the face and other aspects
of the perpetrator's physical appearance and bearing, stores that informa-

---

[14]National Research Council, *Strengthening Forensic Science in the United States: A Path
Forward* (Washington, DC: The National Academies Press, 2009), p. 12.

[15]Police Executive Research Forum, "A National Survey of Eyewitness Identification Procedures in Law Enforcement Agencies," March 2013, p. 48. The survey indicates that 94.1
percent of responding law enforcement agencies reported that they use photo arrays, while
only 21.4 percent reported using live lineups. Sixty-one point eight percent of agencies reported that they use showups. See also J. S. Neuschatz et al., "Comprehensive Evaluation of
Showups," in *Advances in Psychology and Law*, ed. M. Miller and B. Bornstein (New York:
Springer, in press).

[16]Throughout the report, unless otherwise specified, references to *lineups* refer to both photo
arrays and live lineups.

[17]Police Executive Research Forum, p. 65.

tion in memory, and later retrieves the information for comparison with the visual percept of an individual in a lineup. Recent years have seen great advances in our scientific understanding of the basic mechanisms, operational strategies, and limitations of human vision and memory. These advances inform our understanding of the accuracy of eyewitness identification.

Human vision does not capture a perfect, error-free "trace" of a witnessed event. What an individual actually perceives can be heavily influenced by bias[18] and expectations derived from cultural factors, behavioral goals, emotions, and prior experiences with the world. For eyewitness identification to take place, perceived information must be encoded in memory, stored, and subsequently retrieved. As time passes, memories become less stable. In addition, suggestion and the exposure to new information may influence and distort what the individual believes she or he has seen.

Several factors are known to affect the fidelity of visual perception and the integrity of memory. In particular, vision and memory are constrained by processing bottlenecks and various sources of noise.[19] Noise comes from a variety of sources, some associated with the structure of the visual environment, some inherent in the optical and neuronal processes involved, some reflecting sensory content not relevant to the observer's goals, and some originating with incorrect expectations derived from memory. The concept of noise has profound significance for understanding eyewitness identification, as the accuracy of information about the environment gained through vision and stored in memory is necessarily, and often sharply, limited by noise.

The recognition of one person by another—a seemingly commonplace and unremarkable everyday occurrence—involves complex processes that are limited by noise and subject to many extraneous influences. Eyewitness identification research confronts methodological challenges that some other basic experimental sciences do not encounter, as well as practical challenges

---

[18]*Bias* is defined as any tendency that prevents unprejudiced consideration of a question (see Dictionary.com; http://dictionary.reference.com/browse/bias). *Response bias* is a general term for a wide range of influences that moderate the responses of participants away from an accurate or truthful response. Response bias can be induced or caused by a number of factors, all relating to the idea that humans do not respond passively to stimuli, but rather actively integrate multiple sources of information to generate a response in a given situation [(see M. Orne, "On the Social Psychology of the Psychological Experiment: With Particular Reference to Demand Characteristics and Their Implications," *American Psychologist* 17: 776–783, (1962)]. In research, bias is seen in sampling or testing when circumstances select or encourage one outcome or answer over another (see Merriam-Webster.com; http://www.merriam-webster.com/dictionary/bias).

[19]*Noise* refers here to factors that cause uncertainty on the part of an individual about whether a particular signal (e.g. a specific visual stimulus) is present. This use of the term follows the definition used in electronic signal transmission, in which noise refers to random or irrelevant elements that interfere with detection of coherent and informative signals.

in establishing adequate experimental controls over the numerous variables that affect visual perception and memory.

APPLIED RESEARCH ON EYEWITNESS IDENTIFICATION: SYSTEM AND ESTIMATOR VARIABLES

Our understanding of the underlying processes and limits of eyewitness identification, derived from basic research on vision and memory, is complemented by research directed specifically at the problem of eyewitness identification. The modern era of eyewitness identification research began in the 1970s. Today, eyewitness identification is generally viewed as a behavioral output. The accuracy and reliability of eyewitness identification are critically modulated by variables that include a witness' extant cognition and memory and related psychological and situational factors at the time of the event, over the ensuing intervals, and at all stages of recall (see Figure 1-1). Because a crime is an unexpected event, one can draw a natural distinction between variables that reflect the witness' unplanned situational or cognitive state at the time of the crime and the variables that reflect controllable conditions and internal states following the witnessed events. Researchers categorize these factors, respectively, as *estimator variables* and *system variables*.[20]

System variables describe the characteristics of specific procedures and practices (e.g., the content and nature of instructions given to witnesses who are asked if they are able to make an identification). The criminal justice system can exert some control over system variables by following standardized procedures that are based on scientific knowledge and strengthened through education and training.

One important category of system variables concerns the conditions and protocols for lineup identification. Under current law enforcement practice, eyewitness identification procedures involve having a witness view individuals or images of individuals. Research indicates that accuracy and reliability of eyewitness identifications may be influenced by the type of presentation (e.g., lineup) used, the likeness of non-suspect lineup participants (fillers) to the suspect, the number of fillers, and the suspect's physical location in the presentation.[21,22] Eyewitness performance may be affected by how the lineup images are presented—simultaneously (as a group) or

---

[20]G. L. Wells, "Applied Eyewitness-Testimony Research: System Variables and Estimator Variables," *Journal of Personality and Social Psychology* 36(12):1546–1557 (1978).

[21]N. K. Steblay et al., "Eyewitness Accuracy Rates in Police Showup and Lineup Presentations: A Meta-Analytic Comparison," *Law and Human Behavior* 27(5): 523–540 (October 2003).

[22]R. J. Fitzgerald et al., "The Effect of Suspect-Filler Similarity on Eyewitness Identification Decisions: A Meta-analysis," *Psychology, Public Policy, and Law* 19(2): 151–164 (May 2013).

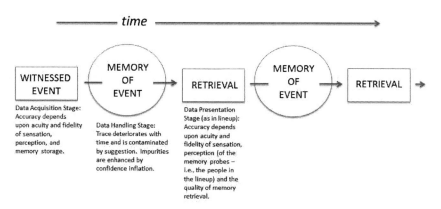

FIGURE 1-1 Memory accuracy and time.
SOURCE: Courtesy of Thomas D. Albright.

sequentially (one at a time). System variables, such as the nature of the instructions and feedback provided before and after the identification procedure, may also affect the eyewitness' identification.

Estimator variables affect the accuracy of eyewitness identification, but they are beyond the control of the criminal justice system. Estimator variables tend to be associated with characteristics of the witness or factors that are operating either at the time of the criminal event (perhaps relating to memory encoding) or the retention interval (the time between witnessing an event and the identification process). Specific examples include the eyewitness' level of stress or trauma at the time of the incident, the light level and nature of the visual conditions that affect visibility and the clarity of a perpetrator's features, and the physical distance between the witness and the perpetrator. Both system and estimator variables will be discussed in detail in subsequent chapters.

EFFORTS AT IMPROVEMENT

In response to insights gained from research on erroneous convictions, there have been attempts to provide recommendations for improving the reliability and validity of eyewitness identifications. An effort of particular note is the National Institute of Justice's (NIJ) Technical Working Group for Eyewitness Evidence (TWGEYEE). Called together by then-U.S. Attorney General Janet Reno in 1998, members of the working group were asked to develop and publish guidance for improving eyewitness identification procedures.[23] The working group recognized the role that memory plays in the mistaken interpretation and remembrance of events and offered guidance based on the practical experiences of the law enforcement community and insights gained from behavioral and psychological research. The NIJ provided detailed instructions for each step of the eyewitness identification procedure to the approximately 18,000 state and local law enforcement agencies across the nation. After the report was issued, only a few states conducted evaluations and engaged in improvement efforts, including the implementation of new laws and the issuance of corrective guidelines and policies. Consequently, eyewitness identification policies remain fragmented by jurisdiction, except in a minority of states that have adopted state-wide policies. At present, the United States does not have a uniform national set of protocols.[24]

JUDICIAL CONSIDERATION OF EYEWITNESS IDENTIFICATION EVIDENCE

The U.S. Supreme Court's 1977 ruling in *Manson v. Brathwaite* provides the current framework for judicial review of eyewitness identification under the Due Process Clause of the U.S. Constitution.[25] The *Manson v. Brathwaite* test asks judges to evaluate the "reliability" of eyewitness identifications using factors derived from prior rulings and not from empirically validated sources. The *Manson v. Brathwaite* ruling was not based on much of the research conducted by scientists on visual perception, memory, and eyewitness identification, and it fails to include important advances that have strengthened standards for judicial review of eyewitness identification evidence at the state level.

In 2011, the Justices of the Massachusetts Supreme Judicial Court convened the Study Group on Eyewitness Identification to "offer guidance as to how our courts can most effectively deter unnecessarily suggestive identification procedures and minimize the risk of a wrongful conviction." The report made five recommendations to minimize inaccurate identifications: (1) acknowledge variables affecting identification accuracy; (2) develop a model policy and implement best practices for police departments; (3) expand use of pretrial hearings; (4) expand use of improved jury instructions; and (5) offer continuing education.[26]

---

[23]U.S. Department of Justice, Office of Justice Programs, *Eyewitness Evidence: A Guide for Law Enforcement* (Washington, DC, 1999).

[24]Police Executive Research Forum, p. 65.

[25]*Manson v. Brathwaite*, 432 U.S. 98, 114 (1977).

[26]Massachusetts Supreme Judicial Court Study Group on Eyewitness Identification, *Report and Recommendations to the Justices*, July 24, 2013, available at: http://www.mass.gov/courts/docs/sjc/docs/eyewitness-evidence-report-2013.pdf.

In 2011, the New Jersey Supreme Court issued a unanimous decision in *State v. Larry R. Henderson*. The opinion revised the legal framework for evaluating and admitting eyewitness identification evidence and directed that improved jury instructions be prepared to help jurors evaluate such evidence. *Henderson* drew on an extensive review of scientific evidence regarding human vision, memory, and the various factors that can affect the reliability of eyewitness identifications. In July 2012, the court released expanded jury instructions and revised court rules relating to eyewitness identifications in criminal cases.[27]

In fall 2012, the Oregon Supreme Court also established a new procedure for evaluating whether eyewitness identifications could be used in court. In *State v. Lawson*, the Court reviewed eyewitness identification research conducted over the past 30 years, determined that the *Manson v. Brathwaite* test "does not accomplish its goal of ensuring that only sufficiently reliable identifications are admitted into evidence," and offered a revised procedure that requires the court to make a determination of whether investigators used "suggestive" tactics to get an identification and the extent to which other information supports the identification.[28]

Despite these improvements and judicial decisions, policies and practices across the country remain inconsistent.

ORGANIZATION OF THE REPORT

This report begins with a description of law enforcement protocols for eyewitness identification (Chapter 2). Chapter 3 presents the legal framework for eyewitness identification evidence. A discussion of the current scientific understanding of visual perception and memory follows in Chapter 4. In Chapter 5, the committee provides an assessment of eyewitness identification research. The report concludes with the committee's findings and recommendations (Chapter 6).

---

[27]New Jersey Judiciary, "Supreme Court Releases Eyewitness Identification Criteria for Criminal Cases," July 19, 2012, available at: http://www.judiciary.state.nj.us/pressrel/2012/pr120719a.htm.

[28]*State v. Lawson*, 352 Or. 724 (Or. 2012).

2

Eyewitness Identification Procedures

Police in the United States investigate millions of crimes each year.[1] Only a small percentage of the police-investigated crimes involve the use of police-arranged identification procedures. Identification procedures are unnecessary when, for example, the perpetrator is caught during the commission of the criminal act, as in the crime of driving while intoxicated, or when the victim knows the perpetrator, as in crimes of domestic violence.[2]

Police use identification procedures for numerous reasons. In some circumstances, the police identify a suspect during an investigation and use the identification procedure to test a witness' ability to identify the suspect as the perpetrator. In other instances, the identification procedure is used as an investigative tool to further an investigation. A positive identification might form probable cause for a search warrant or the apprehension and subsequent questioning of a suspect, or both. Most significant for the purposes of this report are the circumstances in which a witness positively identifies the police suspect as the perpetrator, and the identification serves as compelling evidence in the prosecution of a case.

Data on the number of eyewitness identification procedures are not systematically or uniformly collected. While the exact number of eyewitness

---

[1] Federal Bureau of Investigation, "Crime in the United States 2012: Persons Arrested," available at: http://www.fbi.gov/about-us/cjis/ucr/crime-in-the-u.s/2012/crime-in-the-u.s.-2012/persons-arrested/persons-arrested.

[2] Throughout Chapter 2, the terms *law enforcement* and *police* are used interchangeably and refer to all law enforcement agencies at the local, state, and federal levels.

identification procedures related to crimes involving strangers is unknown, mistaken identifications have disastrous effects for those wrongly accused of crimes and for society should a guilty person go free. Mistaken identifications may also erode public confidence in the criminal justice system as a whole.[3] Recently, some police departments and prosecutors have implemented stringent eyewitness identification procedures in an effort to reduce erroneous convictions.[4]

Police-arranged eyewitness identification procedures vary greatly depending on the nature of the case. In some cases, a police-arranged identification is conducted at the very early stages of an investigation. For instance, consider the circumstance in which police respond to a bank robbery in progress. The perpetrator is described as a white male, approximately 6 feet, 2 inches in height wearing an orange shirt. As the police arrive at the crime scene, an officer observes and apprehends a man fleeing the bank wearing an orange shirt and exhibiting similar physical characteristics. In this situation, a police-arranged identification procedure may be conducted on the scene and prior to any significant investigation. At the other extreme are, for example, lengthy homicide or rape cases that include extensive investigations, forensic testing, and eyewitness interviews conducted over a protracted period of time. Such efforts may culminate in the identification of a suspect and the suspect's inclusion in a photo array identification procedure. In such a circumstance, an eyewitness may not be asked to identify a perpetrator until months after the commission of the crime—and often after repeated probes of her or his memory by, for example, police, family members, and others.

Identification procedures may be used in different ways for different purposes. They are not always used to identify an unknown perpetrator of a crime. The police may, for example, use photo arrays and confirmatory single photographs to clarify the legal identity (birth name/government name) of an individual who is well known to a witness, but only by a street name. In such examples, a witness may know (and may have known) the perpetrator for years but may only be able to identify him by a common

---

[3]See, generally, The International Association of Chiefs of Police, "National Summit on Wrongful Convictions: Building a Systemic Approach to Prevent Wrongful Convictions," August 2013.

[4]See The Innocence Project, *Eyewitness Identification*, available at: http://www.innocence project.org/fix/Eyewitness-Identification.php; U.S. Department of Justice, Office of Justice Programs, *Eyewitness Evidence: A Guide for Law Enforcement* (Washington, DC, 1999); Metropolitan Police—District of Columbia, *General Order—Procedures for Obtaining Pretrial Eyewitness Identification*, April 18, 2013; New York State District Attorneys Association Best Practice Committee, *New York State Photo Identification Guidelines*, October 2010; Rhode Island Police Chiefs Association, *Lineup and Showup Procedures (Eyewitness Identification)*, November 2011; and Innocence Project of Texas, *Eyewitness Identification Reform*, available at: http://www.ipoftexas.org/eyewitness-id.

street name, such as "Prince." The police typically will use an identification procedure to identify the "Prince" to which the witness is referring before they make an arrest or take other investigative measures such as the execution of a search warrant.

This chapter reviews the eyewitness identification procedures commonly used by the police and concludes with a brief discussion of situations in which citizens engage in identifying perpetrators without police assistance.

PHOTOGRAPHIC ARRAY

The photo array is the most common police-arranged identification procedure used in the United States.[5] A photo array consists of six to nine photographs displayed to a witness. An officer might create an array by selecting photographs of persons deemed to resemble the perpetrator.[6] Officers might then display the photographs one at a time to the witness and ask whether she or he recognizes each one. This method is known as a sequential procedure. Officers might also create photo arrays by cutting six square holes in a folder and taping the photographs to the back of the folder so that the faces of the fillers (non-suspects) and suspect are displayed together. When such photographs are presented simultaneously as a two by three matrix, this type of array is referred to as a "six pack." When, as in this instance, photographs are displayed together, this is referred to as a simultaneous procedure.

In 1999, Attorney General Janet Reno released the U.S. Department of Justice, *Eyewitness Evidence: A Guide for Law Enforcement*,[7] one of the earliest efforts to establish standardized procedures for police-arranged eyewitness identification. The guide set forth rigorous criteria and basic procedures to promote accuracy in eyewitness evidence.[8] However, after the guide was released, most police departments in the United States did not adopt these procedures.

Today, many police departments use computer systems to access image databases and assemble photo arrays. Officers enter physical characteristics (e.g., race, gender, hair color) specific to the suspect into a computer, and the system retrieves filler photographs with the desired attributes. If an officer determines that a photograph in the array is suggestive or otherwise inappropriate, she or he can reject one or more fillers and instruct the system

---

[5]Police Executive Research Forum, "A National Survey of Eyewitness Identification Procedures in Law Enforcement Agencies," March 2013, p. 48.

[6]Historically, the photographs were mug shots in the possession of a police department.

[7]U.S. Department of Justice, Office of Justice Programs, *Eyewitness Evidence: A Guide for Law Enforcement* (Washington, DC, 1999).

[8]Ibid, pp. 11–38.

to provide alternate photographs. Departments may conduct the procedure without revealing to the witness how many photographs she or he will view.

In recent decades, many police agencies and prosecutors have adopted sequential presentation of photographs, based on the belief that this approach improves the performance of an eyewitness. Currently, however, there is no consensus among law enforcement professionals as to whether the sequential presentation procedure is superior to the simultaneous procedure (see Chapter 5). The District of Columbia Metropolitan Police Department, for example, does not endorse either simultaneous or sequential procedures in its *Procedures for Obtaining Pretrial Eyewitness Identification.*[9] The District Attorneys Association of the State of New York in 2010 adopted recommended policies for New York State and endorsed the simultaneous method.[10] On the other hand, in North Carolina, legislation was passed that requires that lineup photographs be presented sequentially,[11] and in Massachusetts, the Supreme Judicial Court Study Group on Eyewitness Identification recommended sequential procedures as best practice for Massachusetts Police Departments.[12]

The committee was presented with information regarding improvement efforts from states including New Jersey, Oregon, Rhode Island, Texas, New York, and Massachusetts. However, the committee is unable to determine the percentage of police departments that have adopted policies for eyewitness identification procedures and instituted training in these procedures.[13] Some police departments require that photo arrays be presented to the witness during a procedure that is either "double blind" or "blinded."[14] (See Box 2-1 for a discussion of blinding as used in scientific practice and blinding as used in eyewitness identification procedures.) Blinding is used to prevent conscious and unconscious cues from being given to the witness. In a double-blind procedure, an individual who does not know the identity of the suspect or the suspect's position in the photo array shows a photo array to the eyewitness. In cases where such a double-blind procedure is

---

[9]See Metropolitan Police—District of Columbia, *General Order—Procedures for Obtaining Pretrial Eyewitness Identification*, April 18, 2013.

[10]See New York State District Attorneys Association Best Practice Committee, *New York State Photo Identification Guidelines*, October 2010.

[11]N.C. Gen. Stat. § 15A-284.52 (West 2007).

[12]See Massachusetts Supreme Judicial Court Study Group on Eyewitness Identification, *Report and Recommendations to the Justices* (2013).

[13]The Police Executive Research Forum's 2013 survey of eyewitness identification procedures in law enforcement agencies [Police Executive Research Forum, *A National Survey of Eyewitness Identification Procedures in Law Enforcement Agencies*, (2013)], notes that most agencies that completed the survey have no written policy for eyewitness identification procedures and that more agencies provide training to their employees than have written policies. See pp. 79–80.

[14]Police Executive Research Forum, p. 64.

not feasible, a "blinded" procedure will approximate the condition of double-blinding. For example, the photo array may be administered by an individual who knows who the suspect is, but is unable to tell when the witness is looking at the suspect's photo and so is unable to provide even subconscious feedback to the witness. In one common "blinded" procedure, the officer places each photo in a separate envelope or folder and then shuffles the envelopes/folders so that only the witness sees the images therein. Additional recommendations to minimize the possibility of biasing feedback to the witness include requiring that the officer read instructions to the witness from a pre-printed form.[15]

If the witness identifies someone from the photo array, some departments ask the witness for a confidence statement. Based upon information presented to the committee, it appears that police departments do not always document identification procedures in instances when an identification is not made. Further, if a witness does make an identification, practices differ as to how such information is documented and preserved. Some agencies, for example, require officers to document this information in a written report. Others make audio or video recordings of the identification procedure.

LIVE LINEUP

A live lineup is a police-arranged identification procedure in which the physical suspect and fillers stand or sit in front of the witness (either individually, i.e., sequentially or en masse, i.e., simultaneously). The police generally use at least five fillers. Fillers are selected for their physical similarities to the suspect (gender, race, hair length and color, facial hair, height, skin tone, and other distinguishing features). The fillers are presumed to be unknown to the witness. Traditionally, the suspect and fillers are seated or stood in a row, and the witness views the lineup from behind a two-way mirror. Police use both simultaneous and sequential procedures for live lineups.

Live lineups are used in some jurisdictions, but they are not the predominant method used by law enforcement.[16] The use of these police identification procedures is limited for a variety of reasons. First, in certain circumstances, legal counsel may be required at a lineup, thereby making it less attractive to police and prosecutors. Second, in smaller jurisdictions, it may be difficult to obtain suitable fillers (e.g., those with appropriate

---

[15]As discussed in Chapter 3, the courts have been sensitive to the potential for misidentification resulting from "suggestive" identification procedures and have set standards for admissibility of evidence.

[16]Police Executive Research Forum, p. 48.

BOX 2-1
Blinding

Empirical evidence[a] has shown that the beliefs, desires, and expectations of researchers can influence, often subconsciously, how they observe and interpret the phenomena they study and thus the outcomes of experiments. This evidence has influenced how scientists carry out their experiments, resulting in the use of blind or double-blind procedures to control for this form of bias. Blind assessment[b] has been used since the late 18th century; an early medical trial in 1835 used double-blind assessment, and psychologists started using blinding in the 20th century.[c] By the 1950s, blind assessment in randomized controlled trials was considered standard procedure in both psychological and medical research. Currently, virtually all of science uses some form of blinding.

In single-blind experiments, participants do not know which treatment they are receiving; this form of blinding is used widely across scientific fields. In experiments involving humans, as in medical or psychological research, double-blind procedures are used to guard against "expectancy effects" for both participants and researchers. In a classic double-blind clinical trial, some patients receive active medication and others are given an alternative (either a "standard treatment" or a similar-looking placebo without active ingredients), but neither researchers nor participants know who is receiving which treatment.

In an eyewitness identification setting, double-blinding can be used to prevent a lineup administrator from either intentionally or unintentionally influencing a witness. In these cases, neither the eyewitness nor the administrator knows which persons in a photo array or live lineup are the suspected culprits and which are the fillers.[d,e] In eyewitness identification procedures, as in science, the purpose of double-blinding is to prevent the conscious or subconscious expectations of the administrator from influencing the witness or research outcomes.

In a double-blind photo array, the officer or detective conducting the investigation reads a set of standard instructions to the witness. The instructions may include an advisory that the officer about to show the photos does not know whether any of the photos are of the person who committed the crime. The officer then leaves the room and a second officer—perhaps a patrol officer—displays the

physical similarities to the suspect). Third, conducting a lineup requires a significant amount of time and labor,[17] thereby making photo arrays a more attractive alternative that may be undertaken promptly and with less demand on department resources.

---

[17]Live lineup construction may be further constrained by the inability to hold a suspect in custody without probable cause. See Chapter 3.

photos. It is the duty of this second officer (the "blind administrator") to show the photos and, if an identification is made, document what the witness said and ask the witness how certain she or he is of their identification. Once all photos have been shown, the officer reports the result of the procedure to the investigating officer (preferably out of earshot from the witness).

As an alternative to a double-blind array, some departments use "blinded" procedures. A blinded procedure prevents an officer from knowing when the witness is viewing a photo of the suspect, but can be conducted by the investigating officer. A common approach is the so-called "folder shuffle." With a six-photo array, an officer uses eight manila folders. A photograph of a filler is placed in the top folder, and a photograph of the suspect and four additional fillers are placed in the next five folders. The six folders are then shuffled so that the officer does not know which folder contains the image of the suspect. Two folders with blank paper are placed on the bottom of the stack so that the witness is led to believe that there are more than six images in the array (this is referred to as back-loading, and it prevents the witness from knowing when she or he is about to view the last photograph). After reading instructions to the witness, the administering officer sits to the witness' left and hands him or her one folder at a time and instructs him/her to open each folder and look at the enclosed photo. The cover of the folder blocks the officer from viewing the photo that the witness is viewing. When an identification occurs, the officer notes the witness' words and reaction and asks about the witness' confidence in his or her identification.

---

[a]R. Rosenthal, *Experimenter Effects in Behavioral Research* (New York: John Wiley, 1976).

[b]M. Stolberg, "Inventing the Randomized Double-Blind Trial: The Nürnberg Salt Test of 1835," *James Lind Library Bulletin* (2006), available at: http://www.jameslindlibrary.org/illustrating/articles/inventing-the-randomized-double-blind-trial-the-nurnberg-salt.

[c]T. J. Kaptchuk," Intentional ignorance: A History of Blind Assessment and Placebo Controls in Medicine,\" *Bulletin of the History of Medicine* 72(3): 389–433 (1998).

[d]P. Kilmartin, Presentation to the committee, February 6, 2014.

[e]K. Hamann, Presentation to the committee, December 2, 2013.

SHOWUP

A showup is a police-arranged identification procedure in which the police show one person to a witness and ask if she or he recognizes that person. This procedure typically is used when the police locate a suspect shortly after the commission of a crime and within close proximity to the scene. Case law limits the time and distance from a crime during which such a procedure will pass legal standards. In response to such case law, police typically restrict showups to a two-hour time period after the commission of a crime. Ideally, officials take the witness to the location where the suspect has been detained and do not display the suspect in a suggestive manner (e.g., not in a police car, not handcuffed, without drawn weapons). However, as chases, fights, or disarmaments frequently precede showups, the apprehension of a suspect can raise safety issues that make it difficult to adhere to recommended procedures. Further, the nature of a showup does not lend itself to the use of a blinded procedure. A showup is designed to promptly clear innocent suspects, thereby sparing them from a prolonged period of detention as the investigation continues. Delaying the showup to locate an uninvolved officer may defeat that purpose. While some law enforcement agencies use a standard procedure with written instructions when conducting a showup, there is no indication that such procedures are used uniformly. Courts consider showups highly suggestive, and prosecutors urge the police to exercise caution when conducting them.

CONFIRMATORY PHOTOGRAPH

Police will, on occasion, display a single photograph to a witness in an effort to confirm the identity of a perpetrator. Police typically limit this method to situations in which the perpetrator is previously known to or acquainted with the witness.

FIELD VIEW

Police also use field views in attempts to identify perpetrators. The method, which involves inviting a witness to view many people in a context where the perpetrator is thought likely to appear, is used when the police do not have a suspect but believe that the offender frequents a particular location. For example, police investigating a purse snatching may obtain information that the perpetrator frequents a particular recreation site during the lunch hour. A plainclothes officer or investigator might take the eyewitness to the site and walk around with him or her during the lunch hour without directing his or her attention to any specific individual.

OTHER PROCEDURES—MUG BOOKS AND YEARBOOKS

At times, police use other means to identify perpetrators. In the past, police sometimes had witnesses review mug shot books. Mug books have since been largely replaced by digitized images displayed on computer screens. Nonetheless, there are situations in which the police will have a witness review a large collection of photographs in an effort to identify a perpetrator. Witnesses who identify a perpetrator as being a student at a specific school might be asked to review a yearbook for that school in an effort to identify the perpetrator. When using this method, police typically attempt to mask the names of the students. Similarly, if the offender is believed to be an individual from a certain profession, then the police might have the witness review photographs from the suspect's professional society. Social media sites also serve as the catalyst for police-arranged identification procedures. If a witness knows that the perpetrator is a "friend" of Jane Doe through social media, then the police might have the witness review all friends of Jane Doe to see if she or he recognizes the individual.

All of these additional procedures (i.e., confirmatory photo, field view, mug books, yearbooks) have the potential to introduce biases of the sort that blind lineup procedures are designed to avoid.

NON-POLICE IDENTIFICATION PROCEDURES

In some cases, the victims or witnesses, or both, identify suspects without involving the police. A private citizen, organization, or corporation may conduct an investigation before, during, or even after reporting a crime to the police. The identification of suspects by entities other than law enforcement has become increasingly common as more businesses and private citizens use security cameras to identify criminal actors. High-resolution cameras coupled with high-capacity hard drives allow for real-time streaming of video with superior clarity. Such systems are relatively inexpensive and within financial reach of many home and business owners. Additionally, the proliferation of smart phones has put the ability to create a spontaneous, high-quality video record of an event into the hands of more and more people.

The rise of social media has resulted in the rise of private investigations and identifications using this resource. In one recent case, a stabbing victim drew a picture of her assailant and showed it to her husband.[18] Upon viewing the picture, the husband believed that the assailant looked familiar and might be his ex-girlfriend. He obtained several photographs of the ex-girlfriend from her personal website and showed them to the victim who, after looking at those and other online images, identified the suspect at a lineup and at trial.

CONCLUSION

Many local, state, and federal law enforcement agencies have adopted policies and practices to address the issue of misidentification. However, efforts are not uniform or systemic.[19] Many agencies are unfamiliar with

---

[18]*New Jersey v. Chen*, 27 A.3d 930 (N.J. 2011).
[19]See Massachusetts Supreme Judicial Court Study Group on Eyewitness Evidence, p. 2.

the science that has emerged during the past few decades of research on eyewitness identifications. Questions remain about the optimal design of photo array procedures, including the size of the array, the contents of the photographs, and their relationship to the context of the crime scene. Similar questions apply to the design of live lineups.[20] Eyewitness identification is further complicated by the increasing number of situations in which victims and witnesses seek to identify the perpetrator of a crime without the aid of law enforcement. Such identifications raise new concerns about reliability and accuracy of the identification of individuals. Inconsistent and nonstandard practices might easily add noise to the eyewitness identification process, contaminate the witness, and bias the outcome of an identification procedure.

---

[20]The design of a live lineup is subject to more practical constraints than a photo array.

3

The Legal Framework for Assessment of Eyewitness Identification Evidence

The admissibility of eyewitness testimony at a criminal trial may be challenged on the basis of procedures used by law enforcement officials in obtaining the eyewitness identification. The U.S. Supreme Court, in its 1977 ruling in *Manson v. Brathwaite,* set out the modern test under the Due Process Clause of the U.S. Constitution that regulates the fairness and the reliability of eyewitness identification evidence.[1] The Court also specified five reliability factors, discussed below, that a judge must consider when deciding whether to exclude the identification evidence at trial.[2]

Although the constitutional standards for assessing eyewitness testimony have remained unchanged in the decades since the *Manson v. Brathwaite* decision, a body of research has shed light on the extent to which each of the five reliability factors supports a reliable eyewitness identification. Research has cast doubt, for instance, on the belief that the apparent certainty displayed in the courtroom by an eyewitness is an indicator of an accurate identification, and has found that a number of factors may enhance the certainty of the eyewitness.

Recently, state courts and lower federal courts have taken the lead in developing standards relating to the admissibility of expert evidence, jury instructions, and judicial notice of scientific evidence. Some states have adopted more stringent standards for regulating eyewitness identification evidence than the U.S. Constitution requires, either by legislative statutes or by state court decisions, and have modified or entirely supplanted the *Man-*

---

[1] *Manson v. Brathwaite*, 432 U.S. 98, 113–114 (1977).
[2] *Manson v. Brathwaite* at 114.

son v. Brathwaite test to take account of advances in the growing body of scientific research. This chapter describes the changes in the legal standards for eyewitness identification and explores the relationship between the state of the scientific research and the law regulating procedures and evidence.

EYEWITNESS EVIDENCE AND DUE PROCESS UNDER THE U.S. CONSTITUTION

Beginning with rulings in 1967, the U.S. Supreme Court set out a standard under the Due Process Clause of the Fourteenth Amendment for reviewing eyewitness identification evidence.[3] In *Manson v. Brathwaite*, the Court emphasized that "reliability is the linchpin in determining the admissibility of identification testimony."[4] First, the Court instructed judges to examine whether the identification procedures were unnecessarily suggestive. Second, to assess whether an identification is reliable, judges were instructed to examine the following five factors: (1) the opportunity of the witness to view the criminal at the time of the crime; (2) the witness' degree of attention; (3) the accuracy of the witness' prior description of the criminal; (4) the level of certainty demonstrated at the confrontation; and (5) the time between the crime and the identification procedure.[5] The five factors were drawn from earlier judicial rulings and not from scientific research.[6]

Eyewitness identification evidence continues to be litigated primarily under the flexible two-part *Manson v. Brathwaite* Due Process test.[7] It is

---

[3]In *Stovall v. Denno*, 388 U.S. 293, 302 (1967), the U.S. Supreme Court first set out a due process rule asking whether identification procedures used were "so unnecessarily suggestive and conducive to irreparable mistaken identification." The Court elaborated that rule in decisions such as *Simmons v. U.S.*, 390 U.S. 377, 384 (1968) and *Foster v. California*, 394 U.S. 440, 442 (1969), and then adopted an approach setting out "reliability" considerations in *Neil v. Biggers*, 409 U.S. 188 (1972). For a description of the development of this doctrine, see, e.g., B. L. Garrett, "Eyewitnesses and Exclusion," *Vanderbilt Law Review* 65(2): 451, 463–467 (2012).

[4]*Brathwaite*, 423 U.S. at 114.

[5]*Id.* at 114.

[6]*Id.* at 114. Justice Thurgood Marshall dissented, noting studies indicated that unnecessarily suggestive eyewitness identifications had resulted in "repeated miscarriages of justice resulting from juries' willingness to credit inaccurate eyewitness testimony." 432 U.S. at 125–27 (Marshall, J., dissenting).

[7]Due process is the most important constitutional right that arises in challenges to eyewitness identification, but rights under the Fourth and Sixth Amendments also may be implicated. The Fourth Amendment protects individuals "against unreasonable searches and seizures," and the probable cause typically required to seize and arrest a suspect may arise from an eyewitness identification. U.S. Const. Amend. IV. The few lower courts to address the question are divided on whether probable cause is needed to place individuals in a live lineup procedure. *Biehunik v. Felicetta*, 441 F.2d 228, 230 (2d Cir. 1971); but see, e.g., *Wise v. Murphy*, 275 A.2d 205, 212–15 (D.C. 1971); *State v. Hall*, 461 A.2d 1155 (N.J. 1983). In contrast,

important to note, however, that the vast majority of criminal cases are settled through plea bargaining. The role that evidence type and strength play in plea bargaining is complex and necessarily difficult to study. Because eyewitness identification evidence may never be tested at trial, it is doubly important for lawyers and judges to understand the credibility of the proffered evidence.[8]

In the most recent U.S. Supreme Court ruling addressing a challenge to an eyewitness identification (*Perry v. New Hampshire*),[9] the Court ruled that a due process analysis was not triggered. In that case, while the police were obtaining a description of the suspect, the eyewitness looked out of the apartment window and recognized the suspect standing outside. The police had not intended to conduct an identification procedure. In those circumstances, the Court ruled that the Due Process Clause does not require a preliminary judicial review of the reliability of an eyewitness identification.[10]

---

probable cause is not required to place a person's photograph in an array, since doing so does not involve a seizure. However, courts may also rule that an illegal stop or seizure renders a subsequent identification inadmissible, absent an "independent" source for the courtroom identification. *U.S. v. Crews*, 445 U.S. 463, 473 (1980).

In addition, the Sixth Amendment provides that, in all criminal prosecutions, the accused has the right "to have the assistance of counsel for his defense." In *United States v. Wade*, the Supreme Court held that, once indicted, a person has a right to have a lawyer present at a lineup, reasoning that the right to counsel applies at all "critical" stages of the criminal process. 388 U.S. 218, 235–37 (1967). However, the Court subsequently held that a photo array procedure, of the type now most commonly used by police agencies, does not implicate the *Wade* right to counsel. *U.S. v. Ash*, 413 U.S. 300, 321 (1973).

[8]As the current report demonstrates, a comparative consideration of evidence value is particularly important in the case of eyewitness identification evidence. Similar consideration should be given when other adjudication mechanisms are used (e.g., bench trials).

[9]*Perry v. New Hampshire*, 132 S. Ct. 716, 718 (2012). In that case, the eyewitness happened to look out her window and see the suspect standing at the crime scene where the police had told him to wait. The Court held that the Due Process Clause did not regulate such a situation, since the police did not intend to conduct an identification procedure. *Id.* at 729. The Court indicated that the reliability of the evidence could be addressed by federal and state evidentiary standards, and added: "In appropriate cases, some States also permit defendants to present expert testimony on the hazards of eyewitness identification evidence." *Id.*

[10]Justice Sotomayor dissented, arguing, "Our due process concern . . . arises not from the act of suggestion, but rather from the corrosive effects of suggestion on the reliability of the resulting identification," and the manner in which "[a]t trial, an eyewitness' artificially inflated confidence in an identification's accuracy complicates the jury's task of assessing witness credibility and reliability." *Perry*, 132 S. Ct. at 731–32 (Sotomayor, J., dissenting). Justice Sotomayor also emphasized: "A vast body of scientific literature has reinforced every concern our precedents articulated nearly a half-century ago." *Id.* at 738.

STATE LAW REGULATION OF EYEWITNESS EVIDENCE

State Supreme Court Standards

Several state supreme courts have altered or supplemented the federal *Manson v. Brathwaite* due process rule to focus more on the effects of suggestion, to emphasize certain factors in specific circumstances,[11] or to focus on showup identifications in particular.[12] New Jersey and Oregon have now supplemented the *Manson v. Brathwaite* test with separate state law standards regulating eyewitness identification evidence.

In 2011, the New Jersey Supreme Court issued a unanimous decision in *State v. Larry R. Henderson* that revised the legal framework for admitting eyewitness identification evidence and directed that revised jury instructions be prepared to help jurors evaluate such evidence.[13] The new framework was based on the record of hearings before a Special Master that considered an extensive review of scientific research regarding eyewitness identifications.[14] The legal framework established by the *Henderson* opinion relies on pretrial hearings to review eyewitness evidence and more comprehensive jury instructions at trial.[15] To obtain a pretrial hearing, a defendant must show some evidence of suggestiveness related to either estimator or system

---

[11]See *State v. Ramirez*, 817 P.2d 774, 780–81 (Utah 1991) (altering three of the reliability factors to focus on effects of suggestion); *State v. Marquez*, 967 A.2d 56, 69–71 (Conn. 2009) (adopting criteria for assessing suggestion); *Brodes v. State*, 614 S.E.2d 766, 771 & n.8 (Ga. 2005) (rejecting eyewitness certainty jury instruction); *State v. Hunt*, 69 P.3d 571, 576 (Kan. 2003) (adopting Utah's five factor "refinement" of the *Biggers* factors); *State v. Cromedy*, 727 A.2d 457, 467 (N.J. 1999) (requiring, when applicable, instruction on cross-racial misidentifications).

[12]See, e.g., *State v. Dubose*, 285 Wis.2d 143, 166 (Wis. 2005); *Commonwealth v. Johnson*, 650 N.E.2d 1257, 1261 (Mass. 1995); *People v. Adams*, 423 N.E.2d 379, 383–84 (N.Y. 1981).

[13]*State v. Henderson*, 27 A.3d 872 (N.J. 2011). The *Henderson* opinion described criticisms of the *Manson v. Brathwaite* test, including that suggestion may itself affect the seeming "reliability" of the identification. *Id.* at 877–78. For examples of scholarly criticism of the *Manson v. Brathwaite* test in light of scientific research, see, e.g., G. L. Wells and D. S. Quinlivan, "Suggestive Eyewitness Identification Procedures and the Supreme Court's Reliability Test in Light of Eyewitness Science: 30 Years Later," *Law and Human Behavior* 33(1): 1, 16 (February 2009); T. P. O'Toole and G. Shay, "*Manson v. Brathwaite* Revisited: Towards a New Rule of Decision for Due Process Challenges to Eyewitness Identification Procedures," *Valparaiso University Law Review* 41(1): 109 (2006).

[14]See Report of the Special Master at 16–17, *State v. Henderson*, No. A-8-08 (N.J. June 18, 2011, available at: http://www.judiciary.state.nj.us/pressrel/HENDERSON%20FINAL%20 BRIEF%20.PDF%20(00621142.pdf.

[15]In the companion case, *State v. Chen*, 27 A.3d 930, 932 (N.J. 2011), the New Jersey Supreme Court took an approach that departed from that of the U.S. Supreme Court in *Perry*, ruling that the defendant may be entitled to a hearing in a case in which the eyewitness identified the defendant using social media, not a police-orchestrated identification procedure.

variables that could lead to mistaken identification.[16] At the pretrial hearing, the State must offer proof that the eyewitness identification is reliable. However, the ultimate burden of proving a "very substantial likelihood of irreparable misidentification" is on the defendant.[17]

In July 2012, the New Jersey Supreme Court released an expanded set of jury instructions and related rules that govern the use of suggestive identifications.[18] The jury instructions state that "[r]esearch has shown that there are risks of making mistaken identifications" and noted that eyewitness evidence "must be scrutinized carefully."[19] Human memory involves three stages—encoding, storage, and retrieval. At "each of these stages, memory can be affected by a variety of factors."[20] The Court identified a set of factors that jurors should consider when deciding whether eyewitness identification evidence is reliable, including estimator variables (e.g., stress, exposure duration, weapon focus, distance, lighting, intoxication, disguises or changed appearance of the perpetrator, time since the incident, and cross-racial effects) and system variables (e.g., lineup composition, fillers, use of multiple viewings, presence of feedback, use of double-blind procedures, and use of showup identifications). The instructions also noted the possible influence of outside opinions, descriptions or identifications by other witnesses, and photographs or media accounts.[21]

In 2012, in *Oregon v. Lawson*, the Oregon Supreme Court established a new procedure for evaluating the admissibility of eyewitness identifications. In a unanimous decision, the Court found "serious questions" about the reliability of eyewitness identification, citing research conducted over the past 30 years.[22] The Court determined that the *Manson v. Brathwaite* two-step process for weighing eyewitness identification "does not accomplish its goal of ensuring that only sufficiently reliable identifications are admitted into evidence," because it relies on an eyewitness' self-reports to determine whether the threshold level of suggestiveness is reached, rendering the identification unreliable.[23] The Court set forth a process that requires the trial court to examine whether investigators used "suggestive"

---

[16]*Henderson*, 27 A.3d. at 878.

[17]*Id.*

[18]New Jersey Criminal Model Jury Instructions, *Identification* (July 19, 2012), available at: http://www.judiciary.state.nj.us/pressrel/2012/jury_instruction.pdf; New Jersey Court Rule 3:11, *Record of an Out-of-Court Identification Procedure* (July 19, 2012), available at: http://www.judiciary.state.nj.us/pressrel/2012/new_rule.pdf; New Jersey Court Rule 3:13-3, *Discovery and Inspection* (July 19, 2012), available at: http://www.judiciary.state.nj.us/pressrel/2012/rev_rule.pdf.

[19]See New Jersey Criminal Model Jury Instructions, *Identification, supra* at 2.

[20]*Id.*

[21]*Id.* at 9.

[22]*State v. Lawson*, 352 Ore. 724 (Or. 2012).

[23]*Id.* at 746–748.

identification procedures and whether other factors, such as estimator variables, may have affected the reliability of the identification.[24] The Court ruled that "intermediate remedies," including the use of expert testimony, should be available even if the trial judge concludes that the identification is admissible. The Court also briefly noted that judges might use "case-specific jury instructions."[25]

Other states continue to explore possible changes to the judicial review of eyewitness identification evidence. In 2013, the Massachusetts Supreme Judicial Court Study Group on Eyewitness Identification offered guidance on the adjudication of eyewitness identification evidence.[26] The report adopted *Lawson*'s approach of taking judicial notice of "certain scientifically-established facts about eyewitness identification."[27] The report recommended that trial judges conduct pretrial hearings to determine whether suggestive identification procedures were used, and if so, whether these procedures impaired the reliability of identification evidence. Pretrial hearings would consider the effects of both estimator variables (relating to viewing at the crime scene) and system variables (relating to the lineup or showup procedures) on the identification. The report also recommended that the state adopt a set of recommended practices for conducting identification procedures, create new model jury instructions on eyewitness identifications, and set limitations on the admissibility of certainty statements and in-court identifications.[28]

State Statutes Regulating Identification Procedures

Judicial rulings regulating admissibility of eyewitness evidence in the courtroom do not specify the identification procedures to be used by law enforcement officials. However, 14 states have adopted legislation regarding eyewitness identification procedures. Of the 14, 11 states (Connecticut, Illinois, Maryland, North Carolina, Ohio, Texas, Virginia, West Virginia, Wisconsin, Utah, and Vermont) have enacted statutes directly requiring that

---

[24]*Id.* at 747–748, 755–756.

[25]*Id.* at 759, 763.

[26]See Massachusetts Supreme Judicial Court Study Group on Eyewitness Evidence, *Report and Recommendations to the Justices* (2013).

[27]*Id.* at 48.

[28]*Id.* at 28. In the courtroom, the eyewitness can easily see where the defendant is sitting. Thus, in-court identifications do not reliably test an eyewitness' memory. Nevertheless, courts have shown great tolerance of in-court identifications, deeming them based on "independent" memory, and even following suggestive out-of-court procedures. Garrett, *Eyewitnesses and Exclusion, supra.* For example, the New York Court of Appeals ruled that "[e]xcluding evidence of a suggestive showup does not deprive the prosecutor of reliable evidence of guilt. The witness would still be permitted to identify the defendant in court if that identification is based on an independent source." *People v. Adams*, 423 N.E.2d 379, 384 (N.Y. 1981).

law enforcement officials adopt written procedures for eyewitness identifications and regulating the particular procedures to be used.[29] Three more states (Georgia, Nevada, and Rhode Island) have passed statutes recommending further study, tasking a group with developing best practices, or requiring some form of written policy.[30]

State statutes typically assert that a trial judge may consider the failure to follow the prescribed procedures as a factor in assessing admissibility and informing the jury. The statutes rarely require that a trial judge exclude such identification evidence from consideration by the jury. However, some of the more detailed statutes, such as those in Ohio, North Carolina, and West Virginia, require that law enforcement officials use particular practices (e.g., eyewitness instructions, a blind administrator). Other statutes require adherence to model policies or guidelines. Utah requires that lineup procedures be recorded. Some jurisdictions and departments also have voluntarily adopted guidelines or policies regulating eyewitness identifications.[31] Several state courts have issued rulings regulating lineup practices (e.g., New Jersey's Supreme Court has required documentation of identification procedures).[32]

AIDING JURORS IN ASSESSMENT OF EYEWITNESS TESTIMONY

Expert Witness Testimony Regarding Eyewitness Identification

The standards for assessing the admissibility of testimony by expert witnesses have undergone great changes in the past two decades. Before 1993, the *Frye* test allowed scientific expert testimony in federal courts if it met the standard of "general acceptance" in the relevant scientific community.[33] In 1993, the Supreme Court, in *Daubert v. Merrell Dow*

---

[29]See Conn. Gen. Stat. § 54-1p (West 2012); 725 Ill. Comp. Stat. § 5/107A-5 (West 2003); Md. Code Ann., Pub. Safety § 3-506 (West 2007); N.C. Gen. Stat. § 15A-284.52 (West 2007); Ohio Rev. Code Ann. § 2933.83 (West 2010); Tex. Code Crim. Proc. Ann. art. 38.20 (West 2011); Utah Code Ann. §77-8-4 (West 1980); Va. Code Ann. §19.2-390.02 (West 2005); Va Code Ann. § 9.1-102.54; 13 V.S.A. § 5581; W. Va. Code Ann. § 62-1E-1 (West 2013); Wis. Stat. § 175.50 (West 2005).

[30]GA. H.R. 352, 149th Gen. Assem., Reg. Sess. (April 20, 2007); Nev. Rev. Stat. § 171.1237 (West 2011); R.I. Gen. Laws § 12-1-16 (West 2012); 2010 Leg. Reg. Sess. (Vt. 2010).

[31]See, e.g., John J. Farmer, Jr., Attorney General of the State of New Jersey, "Letter to All County Prosecutors: Attorney General Guidelines for Preparing and Conducting Photo and Live Lineup Identification Procedures" (April 18, 2001), available at: http://www.state.nj.us/lps/dcj/agguide/photoid.pdf; CALEA Standards for Law Enforcement Agencies: 42.2.11 Lineups, available at: http://www.calea.org/content/standards-titles; International Association of Chiefs of Police, Model Policy: Eyewitness Identification (2010).

[32]*State v. Delgado*, 188 N.J. 48, 63–64, 902 A.2d 888 (2006).

[33]*Frye v. United States*, 54 App. D.C. 46, 293 F. 1013 (1923).

Pharmaceuticals, Inc.,[34] ruled that, under Federal Rule of Evidence 702, a "trial judge must ensure that any and all scientific testimony or evidence admitted is not only relevant, but reliable."[35] Judges determine reliability by assessing the scientific foundation of the expert's testimony prior to trial, so that *"evidentiary reliability* will be based upon *scientific validity."*[36] Many states have adopted *Daubert,* and many of those that have not formally adopted *Daubert* have revised their *Frye* test to adopt much of the *Daubert* standard. In turn, Federal Rule of Evidence 702 has been revised to incorporate the holding in *Daubert.*[37] Federal and state courts remain divided on whether expert testimony on eyewitness identifications is admissible under *Daubert* or *Frye,* and on the proper exercise of trial court discretion when deciding whether to admit such expert testimony. Appellate rulings emphasize that a trial judge should use discretion when deciding whether proffered expert evidence satisfies the *Daubert* or *Frye* standards. An increasing number of rulings emphasize the value of presenting expert testimony regarding eyewitness identification. Some courts have held that it can be an abuse of discretion for a trial judge to bar the defense from admitting such testimony.[38] Detailed descriptions of the relevant scientific research findings accompany such decisions.[39] There are also many federal and state courts that continue to follow the traditional approach, emphasizing that credibility of eyewitnesses is a matter within the "province of the jury" and insisting that information regarding valid scientific research in this area will not assist the jury in its task.[40]

---

[34] 509 U.S. 579 (1993).

[35] *Id.* at 589.

[36] *Id.* at 590 n.9.

[37] Fed. R. Evid. 702. Rule 702 now provides:

A witness who is qualified as an expert by knowledge, skill, experience, training, or education may testify in the form of an opinion or otherwise if: (a) the expert's scientific, technical, or other specialized knowledge will help the trier of fact to understand the evidence or to determine a fact in issue; (b) the testimony is based on sufficient facts or data; (c) the testimony is the product of reliable principles and methods; and (d) the expert has reliably applied the principles and methods to the facts of the case.

[38] See, e.g., *Tillman v. State,* 354 S.W.3d 425, 441 (Tex. Crim. App. 2011); *People v. Le-Grand,* 835 N.Y.S.2d 523, 524 (2007); *State v. Clopten,* 223 P.3d 1103, 1117 (Utah 2009); *U.S. v. Smithers,* 212 F.3d 306, 311–14 (6th Cir. 2000).

[39] See, e.g., *State v. Copeland,* 226 S.W.3d 287, 299–300 (Tenn. 2007); *Tillman,* 354 S.W.3d at 441; *Clopten,* 223 P.3d at 1108.

[40] For scholarly examination of this case law, see, e.g., "The Province of the Jurist: Judicial Resistance to Expert Testimony on Eyewitnesses as Institutional Rivalry," *Harvard Law Review* 126(8): 2381 (2013); R. Simmons, "Conquering the Province of the Jury: Expert Testimony and the Professionalization of Fact-Finding," *University of Cincinnati Law Review* 74: 1013 (2006); G. Vallas, "A Survey of Federal and State Standards for the Admission of Expert Testimony on the Reliability of Eyewitnesses," *American Journal of Criminal Law* 39(1): 97 (2011).

The trend is toward greater acceptance of expert testimony regarding the factors that may affect eyewitness identification. In a 2012 decision, the Connecticut Supreme Court disavowed earlier rulings restricting expert testimony and stated that such rulings are now "out of step with the widespread judicial recognition that eyewitness identifications are potentially unreliable in a variety of ways unknown to the average juror."[41] Similarly, the Pennsylvania Supreme Court recently held that expert testimony on eyewitness identifications was no longer *per se* inadmissible, emphasizing that "courts in 44 states and the District of Columbia have permitted such testimony at the discretion of the trial judge," and that "all federal circuits that have considered the issue, with the possible exception of the 11th Circuit, have embraced this approach."[42] As the Seventh Circuit Court of Appeals recently explained:

> It will not do to reply that jurors know from their daily lives that memory is fallible. The question that social science can address is how fallible, and thus how deeply any given identification should be discounted. That jurors have beliefs about this does not make expert evidence irrelevant; to the contrary, it may make such evidence vital, for if jurors' beliefs are mistaken then they may reach incorrect conclusions. Expert evidence can help jurors evaluate whether their beliefs about the reliability of eyewitness testimony are correct.[43]

Courts also have allowed expert witnesses to testify about particular issues concerning eyewitness identifications, such as cross-race effects, stress, weapons focus, suggestive lineup procedures, and the like.[44] Rarely have experts conducted eyewitness identification research related to the specific case before the court. However, in one such case, in which an experiment

---

[41]*State v. Guilbert*, 306 Conn. 218, 234 (Conn. 2012). Prior to that decision, the Connecticut Supreme Court had long ruled that "the reliability of eyewitness identification is within the knowledge of jurors and expert testimony generally would not assist them in determining the question" (*State v. Kemp, supra* 199 Conn. at 473, 477), and that factors affecting eyewitness memory are "nothing outside the common experience of mankind" (*State v. McClendon, supra* 248 Conn. at 572, 586).

[42]*Com. v. Walker*, 2014 WL 2208139 *13 (Pa. 2014) (collecting authorities).

[43]*U.S. v. Bartless*, 567 F.3d 901, 906 (7th Cir. 2009). Other federal courts have found it a proper exercise of discretion to exclude expert testimony on eyewitness identifications. See, e.g., *United States v. Lumpkin*, 192 F.3d 280, 289 (2d Cir. 1999). Most federal courts treat the subject as one of considerable trial discretion; see, e.g., *United States v. Rodriguez-Berrios*, 573 F.3d 55, 71–72 (1st Cir. 2006). For a survey of federal decisions, see Lauren Tallent, Note, *Through the Lens of Federal Evidence Rule 403: An Examination of Eyewitness Identification Expert Testimony Admissibility in the Federal Circuit Courts*, Washington & Lee Law Review 68 (2): 765 (2011); see also Walker, 2014 2208139 *13.

[44]See, e.g., *Loftus, Doyle & Dysart* at § 14-8[a]-[b] p. 408 n. 41–42, 410, n. 53 (5th Edition, 2013) (collecting cases).

was conducted with the actual photo array used in the case, the federal courts found expert testimony admissible where it was directed not only to general research, but also by the question of whether suggestive procedures affected the identification in that case.[45]

Expert witnesses who explain the complications of eyewitness identification can be expensive. Most criminal defendants are indigent and cannot afford such assistance.[46] In *Ake v. Oklahoma,* the Supreme Court held that an indigent defendant has a constitutional due process right to assistance by an expert witness only if that expert assistance is so crucial to the defense (or such a "significant factor") that its denial would deprive the defendant of a fundamentally fair trial.[47] In federal courts, funding for expert witnesses is available, and requests by indigent defendants are common.[48] In state courts, such assistance is uncommon, especially in state courts that rarely find denial of expert assistance on eyewitness matters to be a due process violation.

Expert testimony on eyewitness memory and identifications has many advantages over jury instructions as a method to explain relevant scientific framework evidence to the jury: (1) Expert witnesses can explain scientific research in a more flexible manner, by presenting only the relevant research to the jury; (2) Expert witnesses are familiar with the research and can describe it in detail; (3) Expert witnesses can convey the state of the research at the time of the trial; (4) Expert witnesses can be cross-examined by the other side; and (5) Expert witnesses can more clearly describe the limitations of the research. The benefits of expert testimony are offset somewhat by the expense. However, conflicting testimony by opposing experts may lead to confusion among the jurors. Nonetheless, trial judges have discretion to determine whether the potential benefits of expert testimony outweigh the cost.

Jury Instructions Regarding Eyewitness Identification

Some courts restricting expert testimony have found jury instructions regarding the fallible nature of eyewitness identifications to be an acceptable substitute for expert testimony.[49] At the conclusion of a criminal trial,

---

[45]*Newsome v. McCabe,* 319 F.3d 301 (7th Cir. 2003).

[46]See, e.g., Bureau of Justice Statistics, "Indigent Defense," available at: http://www.bjs.gov/index.cfm?ty=pbdetail&iid=995.

[47]470 U.S. 68, 82–83 (1985). Even if an indigent defendant receives funding to retain an expert, the judge may ultimately decide that the expert testimony is not admissible at trial.

[48]18 U.S.C. § 3006A(e)(1).

[49]See, e.g., *U.S. v. Jones,* 689 F.3d 12, 20 (1st Cir. 2012) ("The judge was fully entitled to conclude that this general information could be more reliably and efficiently conveyed by instructions rather than through dueling experts.").

the trial judge can instruct jurors on the factors that may result in an erroneous identification while also offering instructions on the legal principles jurors must apply when assessing the factual record. Such instructions may be given when the witness testifies. Judges tend to rely on model or pattern instructions, because any departure from these standard instructions may be a ground for appellate reversal.

The New Jersey Supreme Court viewed jury instructions as preferable to expert testimony.[50] The New Jersey instructions adopted, following the *Henderson* decision, are by far the most detailed set of jury instructions regarding eyewitness identification evidence. Traditionally, instructions regarding eyewitness identifications have been brief and remind the jurors to consider the following: (1) the credibility of an eyewitness is like that of any other witness and (2) any eyewitness identification is part of the prosecutor's burden of proof in a criminal case.[51] Many state courts have held that, although general jury instructions regarding credibility and the burden of proof are appropriate, more specific instructions on eyewitness identifications are considered an inappropriate judicial comment on the evidence.[52] Following the U.S. Supreme Court's decision in *Manson v. Brathwaite,* some state courts supplemented their jury instructions by including the five reliability factors named by the Supreme Court.[53]

In 1972, in *U.S. v. Telfaire,* the D.C. Circuit Court of Appeals adopted a set of influential model jury instructions to be used in appropriate federal cases involving eyewitness identifications.[54] The instructions emphasized the following:

> You must consider the credibility of each identification witness in the same way as any other witness, consider whether he is truthful, and consider

---

[50]The New Jersey Supreme Court indicated: "Jury charges offer a number of advantages: they are focused and concise, authoritative (in that juries hear them from the trial judge, not a witness called by one side), and cost-free; they avoid possible confusion to jurors created by dueling experts; and they eliminate the risk of an expert invading the jury's role or opining on an eyewitness' credibility." *Henderson,* 27 A.3d at 925.

[51]New Jersey courts used such instructions a decade before *Henderson.* See, e.g., *State v. Robinson,* 165 N.J. 32, 46–47 (N.J. 2000). Some states have also approved instructions informing the jury that there may be an "independent source" for an in-court identification. See, e.g., *State v. Cannon,* 713 P.2d 273, 281 (Ariz. 1985).

[52]*Brodes v. State,* 279 Ga. 435, 439 & n.6 (Ga. 2005) (surveying state case law).

[53]*State v. Tatum,* 219 Conn. 721 (1991).

[54]*U.S. v. Telfaire,* 469 F.2d 552, 558 (D.C. Cir. 1972). Some federal courts follow that approach, while others adopt a "flexible approach." See, e.g., *United States v. Luis,* 835 F.2d 37, 41 (2d Cir. 1987). Some more recent federal model instructions include added detail, reflecting variables such as stress and cross-race identifications. See, e.g., Third Circuit Model Criminal Jury Instructions, 4.15 (Jan. 2014), available at: http://www.ca3.uscourts.gov/sites/ca3/files/2013%20Chapter%204%20final%20revised.pdf.

whether he had the capacity and opportunity to make a reliable observation on the matter covered in his testimony.[55]

The *Telfaire* instructions departed from the brief traditional instruction by adding that the jury should consider factors related to the initial sighting, including "how long or short a time was available, how far or close the witness was, how good were lighting conditions, [and] whether the witness had had occasion to see or know the person in the past." The decision also noted that an identification is more reliable if the witness is able to pick the defendant out of a group, rather than at a showup, and that the jury should consider the length of time between the crime and the identification.[56]

Some states have adopted cautionary instructions on specific issues related to eyewitness identification evidence. In *State v. Ledbetter,* the Connecticut Supreme Court ordered lower courts to use a special instruction in cases in which law enforcement failed to instruct the eyewitness that the perpetrator may or may not be present in a lineup.[57] The Georgia Supreme Court concluded in 2005 that one particular use of the *Manson v. Brathwaite* factors must no longer be permitted: "we can no longer endorse an instruction authorizing jurors to consider the witness' certainty in his/her identification as a factor to be used in deciding the reliability of that identification."[58] Other courts have done the same.[59] In 1999, the New Jersey Supreme Court ruled in *State v. Cromedy* that instructions on cross-racial identifications are required in certain cases.[60]

Expert testimony on eyewitness memory and identifications appears to have many advantages when used as a method to explain relevant scientific framework evidence to the jury. However, when expert testimony is not available to the defense, jury instructions may be a preferable alternative means to inform the jury of the findings of scientific research in this area.

---

[55]*U.S. v. Telfaire,* 469 F.2d at 559.

[56]*Id.* at 558.

[57]*State v. Ledbetter,* 275 Conn. 534, 579–580 (2005) (The instruction reads, in part, "the individual conducting the procedure either indicated to the witness that a suspect was present in the procedure or failed to warn the witness that the perpetrator may or may not be in the procedure. Psychological studies have shown that indicating to a witness that a suspect is present in an identification procedure or failing to warn the witness that the perpetrator may or may not be in the procedure increases the likelihood that the witness will select one of the individuals in the procedure, even when the perpetrator is not present. Thus, such behavior on the part of the procedure administrator tends to increase the probability of a misidentification.")

[58]*Brodes,* 279 Ga. at 442.

[59]See, e.g., *supra Commonwealth v. Payne,* 426 Mass. 692 (1998); *State v. Romero,* 191 N.J. 59 (2007).

[60]*State v. Cromedy,* 158 N.J. 112 (1999); see also Innocence Project, "Know the Cases: McKinley Cromedy," available at: http://www.innocenceproject.org/Content/McKinley_Cromedy.php.

Brief instructions may not, however, provide sufficient guidance to explain the relevant scientific evidence to the jury, but lengthy instructions may be cumbersome and complex.

More research is warranted to better understand how best to communicate to jurors the factors that may affect the validity of eyewitness testimony and support a more sensitive discrimination of the strengths and weaknesses of eyewitness testimony in individual cases. Indeed, research findings on the effectiveness of jury instructions on assessment of eyewitness identification evidence have been mixed. In general, such studies find that jury instructions cause jurors to become more suspicious of all eyewitness identification evidence.[61] A recent study of the effect of the New Jersey jury instructions used in *Henderson* found that the instructions reduced juror reliance on *both* strong and weak eyewitness identification evidence.[62] Among the few studies finding that jury instructions succeed in increasing jurors' sensitivity to the strength of such evidence are those that study the effect of jury instructions presented before the eyewitness testimony rather than at the end of the case before deliberation.[63] Such studies also have examined instructions that use visual aids rather than rely on a judge's recitation of written instructions.[64] In addition, research studies might explore the use of videotape as an alternative way to present such information[65] and the effects of moving jury instructions to precede the introduction of the testimony by the eyewitness.

[61]For a review of this research, see K. A. Martire and R. I. Kemp, "The Impact of Eyewitness Expert Evidence and Judicial Instruction on Juror Ability to Evaluate Eyewitness Testimony," *Law and Human Behavior* 33:225–236, 226 (reviewing studies of jury instructions on eyewitness identification and concluding that increased skepticism and confusion is a common result); see also J. L. Devenport, C. D. Kimbrough, and B. L. Cutler, "Effectiveness of traditional safeguards against erroneous conviction arising from mistaken eyewitness identification," in *Expert testimony on the psychology of eyewitness identification*, ed. B. L. Cutler (New York: Oxford University Press, 2009), 51–68 (summarizing research studying the *Telfair* jury instruction and concluding that "cautionary jury instructions may be an ineffective safeguard against erroneous convictions resulting from mistaken eyewitness identifications.").

[62]A. P. Papailiou, D. V. Yokum, C. T. Robertson, "The Novel New Jersey Eyewitness Instruction Induces Skepticism But Not Sensitivity," August 2014, available at: http://papers.ssrn.com/sol3/papers.cfm?abstract_id=2475217.

[63]See, e.g., N. B. Pawlenko, M. A. Safer, R. A. Wise, and B. Holfeld, "A Teaching Aid for Improving Jurors' Assessments of Eyewitness Accuracy," *Applied Cognitive Psychology* 27(2): 190–197. Other studies are reviewed in Martire and Kemp, *supra* note 105 at 226.

[64]Pawlenko et al., *supra* note 107.

[65]For an example of videotaped instructions, see Federal Judicial Center, *The Patent Process: An Overview for Jurors*, available at: *http://www.youtube.com/watch?v=ax7QHQTbKQE*.

CONCLUSION

The *Manson v. Brathwaite* test under the Due Process Clause of the U.S. Constitution set out the modern test that regulates the fairness and the reliability of eyewitness identification evidence. The test evaluates the "reliability" of eyewitness identifications using factors derived from prior rulings and not from empirically validated sources. It includes factors that are not diagnostic of reliability and treats factors such as the confidence of a witness as independent markers of reliability when, in fact, it is now well established that confidence judgments may vary over time and can be powerfully swayed by many factors. The best guidance for legal regulation of eyewitness identification evidence comes not, however, from constitutional rulings, but from the careful use and understanding of scientific evidence to guide fact-finders and decision makers.

4

Basic Research on Vision and Memory

Accurate eyewitness identification requires that a witness to a crime correctly sense, perceive, and remember objects and events that occurred and recall them later. The veracity of the witness' identification thus depends on the limits of sensation, perception, and memory. Recent scientific studies have yielded great advances in our understanding of how vision and memory work. This chapter provides a brief overview of current knowledge, identifies areas in which vision and memory are imperfect, and describes implications for the accuracy of eyewitness identification. These implications, in turn, have guided much of the applied research on this topic (see Chapter 5) and provide a general framework for the recommendations made herein (see Chapter 6).

VISION AND MEMORY IN CONTEXT

This chapter begins by offering a concrete example to place the body of basic scientific research on vision and memory in context so as to better communicate its relevance to eyewitness identification. In the sections that follow the example, the different functional steps of the sequence (highlighted in italics) are dissected in some detail, with special reference to its limitations and the ways in which it may fail to deliver accurate eyewitness identification.

> While returning home late, you hear a muffled scream from around the street corner. Seconds later, you come face-to-face with a man turning the corner and moving swiftly past you. Instantaneously, properties of the

scene are conveyed to you through patterns of light cast on the backs of
your eyes and *sensed by photoreceptors* in your retina. Only a fraction of
the information sensed is selected for further processing; in this case you
focus your attention on certain features of the man's face. Those features
are *integrated and interpreted to yield a coherent percept* of the man.
As you round the corner, you perceive, through an identical process, the
victim slumped lifelessly against a wall. You quickly grasp the meaning of
these perceptual experiences, and they immediately elicit both cognitive
and visceral components (e.g., increased heart rate) of fear and anxiety.
Your percepts are initially *encoded in short-term working memory*, where
content is limited and labile. Your elevated level of arousal may cause
interference and some loss of content, but with time and recognition of
the importance of the experience, your percepts are *consolidated into long-
term memory*. Long-term memories are *maintained in storage* but subject
to ongoing updates and modifications resulting from new experiences and
perhaps distortions caused by sustained levels of stress.

At a later date, you are asked to look at a police lineup that includes a
suspect apprehended near the crime scene. Visual features of the men in the
lineup are *sensed, selectively attended*, and *perceived*, using the same visual
processes engaged on the night in question. Some of these features—the
high brow and sharp cheekbones of one man in the lineup—*elicit retrieval*
of memories of your visual experiences on the night of the crime. The simultaneously perceived and retrieved experiences are implicitly compared,
leading to a cycle of greater visual scrutiny of the man in front of you and
retrieval of additional details of the original percept. The context of the
lineup procedure, the sight of the man, and the retrieved memories trigger
latent emotions and anxiety, which may interfere with your comparison
of percept and memory. Eventually, the comparison reaches your internal
criterion for identification: You decide, with an implicit level of certainty,
that your current visual percept and the percept from the night of the
crime were caused by the same external source (the man now in front of
you), and you assert that you have *identified the person you witnessed at
the crime scene*.

VISION

Functional Processes of Vision

To understand the contributions and limitations of vision to eyewitness identification, it is useful to consider the workings of three functional
stages of visual processing—sensation, attention, and perception—bearing
in mind that they comprise highly interdependent elements of a continuous
operation. *Sensation* is the initial process of detecting light and extracting
basic image features. Sensations themselves are evanescent, and only a small

fraction of what is sensed is actually perceived. *Attention* is the process by which information sensed by the visual system is selected for further processing. *Perception* is the process by which attended visual information is integrated, linked to environmental cause, made coherent, and categorized through the assignment of meaning, utility, value, and emotional valence. In addition, memories and emotions resulting from prior experiences with the world can influence all stages of visual processing and thus define a thread that weaves throughout the following discussions.

All of the functional processes of vision are beset by noise, which affects the quality and types of information accessible from the visual environment, and bears heavily on the validity of eyewitness identification. Before considering the processes of sensation, attention, and perception in greater detail, consideration is given to the concept of noise in visual processing and to ways of interpreting its impact on visual experience.

The Fundamental Role of Noise

Vision is usefully understood as the process of detecting informative signals about the external world and using those signals to recognize objects, make decisions, and guide behavior. As with any signal detection, there are occasionally factors that lead to uncertainty on the part of the observer about whether a particular signal is present. These factors are generically termed *noise*, following the definition used in electronic signal transmission, in which noise refers to random or irrelevant elements that interfere with detection of coherent and informative signals. In vision, noise comes from a variety of sources, some associated with the structure of the visual environment (e.g., occluding surfaces, glare, shadows), some inherent to the optical and neuronal processes involved (e.g., scattering of light in the eye), some reflecting sensory content not relevant to the observer's goals (e.g., a distracting sign or a loud sound), and some originating with incorrect expectations derived from memory. Consider, for example, the seemingly simple problem of detecting a green light while waiting at a traffic signal. In this case, your ability to "see" the green light may be compromised by glare or dust on your windshield, by poor visual acuity, by your eyes having been aimed instead at the driver of the adjacent car, by the presence of other (irrelevant) colored lights in your field of view (e.g., a traffic signal at a different intersection or the lights of a nearby restaurant), by a cell phone conversation, or by the news on the car radio. The significance of this view for eyewitness identification is profound, as it helps us to realize that the accuracy of information about the environment—the face of a criminal, for example—gained through vision is necessarily, and often sharply, limited by noise.[1]

The fact that vision is noise-limited suggests a familiar statistical framework—signal detection theory—for assessing and understanding the effects of noise on visual perception and recognition ability.[2] Signal detection theory has long been successfully applied to analogous problems in electronic signal reception.[3] To illustrate these principles as applied to sensory processing, consider the problem of detecting a vibrating cell phone in your pocket. Anyone who has operated a cell phone in vibrate mode will be familiar with two types of signal detection errors: (1) the occasional sense that the phone is vibrating in your pocket, only to discover that it is not, and, conversely, (2) the phone call that is sometimes missed because you attribute the vibration to some other cause. *Signal*, in this example, is a subtle tactile stimulus resulting from an incoming phone call. *Noise*, in this example, is all of the other things in your environment that may also lead to subtle tactile stimulation, such as vibration of your car seat, a shift of keys in your pocket, or the touch of another person.

Signal detection theory posits that there are three main factors that determine whether a signal will be detected: (1) the distribution of stimuli (e.g., the variety of stimulus magnitudes) that reflect noise only, (2) the distribution of stimuli that reflect signal, and (3) the observer's criterion for "deciding" that a specific stimulus resulted from noise sources or signal. An important factor for the fidelity of signal detection is the degree to which noise and signal distributions overlap with one another. In the case of the vibrating cell phone, if the distributions of tactile stimuli resulting from noise and signal overlap, as is often the case, then there will always be some cases in which you believe the phone is vibrating when it is not (noise stimuli attributed to signal source), and there will be some cases in which the phone is vibrating and you miss the call (signal stimuli attributed to noise source).

The third factor that influences signal detection in the presence of noise is the observer's decision criterion, which is simply the value (e.g., stimulus amplitude) above which a stimulus is attributed to signal, and below which a stimulus is attributed to noise. In the same sense that your car radio is programmed to "decide" (and allow you to hear) when informative patterns of electromagnetic radiation (signal) are sufficiently different from random fluctuations (noise), an observer adopts a criterion for deciding whether a

---

[1] W. S. Geisler, "Sequential Ideal-Observer Analysis of Visual Discriminations," *Psychological Review* 96(2): 267–314 (1989).

[2] D. M. Green and J. A. Swets, *Signal Detection Theory and Psychophysics* (New York: Wiley, 1966).

[3] W. W. Peterson, T. G. Birdsall, and W. C. Fox, "The Theory of Signal Detectability," *Proceedings of the IRE Professional Group on Information Theory* 4(4): 171–212 (1954).

stimulus is caused by a signal or is simply a manifestation of noise. This criterion reflects the level of precision acceptable for the observer's needs, given uncertainty about whether a given stimulus reflects a real signal.

In practice, the criterion[4] used is determined by a host of factors unique to the circumstances, including psychological and social demands and behavioral goals. These factors collectively determine the relative "costs" of incorrect attributions of signal as noise ("misses") and of noise as signal ("false alarms").

If an individual places high value on not missing a phone call, then she or he will adopt a very *liberal* criterion, in which all stimuli reflecting real incoming calls (signal) are successfully detected, but many noise stimuli (e.g., shifting keys in a pocket) are erroneously (and frustratingly) believed to be incoming calls. By contrast, if an individual places little value on detecting incoming phone calls, she or he will adopt a *conservative* criterion, in which many calls are missed and noise stimuli rarely elicit an effort to answer the phone, which may be of value to the individual who wishes to avoid distraction.

The example of the signal detection logic used for the vibrating cell phone applies similarly to all aspects of visual perceptual experience, including the conditions of witnessing criminal events. The uncertainty about visual events caused by manifold sources of noise will inevitably lead to inaccurate visual perceptual experiences, which result from conditions in which an observer fails to detect a critically informative stimulus as "real" (attributing the stimulus instead to a source of noise) or confidently perceives a noise stimulus to have originated from an informative source. The latter instance is problematic because it increases the likelihood that observers will unwittingly "construct," on the basis of expectations derived from memory and situational context, perceptual experiences to account for noise erroneously interpreted as signal.

What follows from this consideration of uncertainty and decision criteria for visual perception is that the actual impact of factors that limit the amount of visual information available to an eyewitness (factors considered in more detail below) will depend on the criterion adopted. The criterion may reflect the values and prejudices of the eyewitness, his or her motivational and emotional state, and a variety of behavioral goals. In principle, the observer's criterion can be altered by instruction or incentives, but it is important to note that the criterion held by an observer witnessing a crime scene cannot be anticipated, nor can it be altered after the fact. It is an "estimator variable," which simply needs to be recognized and understood when evaluating eyewitness reports. By contrast, the decision criterion held

---

[4]The criterion is sometimes referred to as bias.

by an observer at the time of identification can be controlled, and there may be valid reasons for doing so (see Chapter 5).[5]

In the following discussions of sensation, attention, and perception, the various means and conditions under which many different types of noise introduce uncertainty in visual signal detection (and thus fundamentally limit the accuracy of eyewitness identification) are addressed.

Visual Sensation

When an observer views an object of any sort (such as a person) or events involving the object (a criminal act), patterns of light reflected from the environment are focused by the lens at the front of the eye and projected onto the back surface of the eye (the retina) to form the retinal image. Light in the image is initially "sensed" by the activation of photoreceptors, and early stages of sensory processing function to detect spatial and temporal contrast along a number of dimensions, including intensity and wavelength of light.[6] These contrast measurements are integrated by subsequent processing stages in the brain to yield representations of basic image features, or primitives, such as oriented image contours.[7]

Several sources of noise, or factors that limit the ratio of signal to noise, can restrict the visual information accessible to these early sensory processes. Some factors are inherent to the visual system and largely uncontrollable (e.g., the scattering of light by the fluid and tissues of the eye) and can be exacerbated by common observer-specific visual deficits (e.g., myopia, poor contrast sensitivity, or color blindness). Others factors are dependent on viewing conditions (e.g., the effects of viewing time and level of illumination).[8] Both of these types of factors predictably influence the quantity of information—the visual signal strength—that a viewer gains from a visual scene, and thus the degree to which the perceptual experi-

---

[5]L. Mickes, H. D. Flowe, and J. T. Wixted, "Receiver Operating Characteristic Analysis of Eyewitness Memory: Comparing the Diagnostic Accuracy of Simultaneous and Sequential Lineups," *Journal of Experimental Psychology: Applied* 18(4): 361–376 (2012).

[6]M. Meister and M. Tessier-Lavigne, "Low-level Visual Processing: The Retina," in *Principles of Neuroscience*, 5th Edition, ed. E. Kandel, J. H. Schwartz, T. M. Jessell, S. A. Siegelbaum, and A. J. Hudspeth (New York: McGraw-Hill Professional, 2012), 577–601.

[7]C. D. Gilbert, "Intermediate-level Visual Processing and Visual Primitives," in *Principles of Neuroscience*, 5th Edition, ed. E. Kandel, J. H. Schwartz, T. M. Jessell, S. A. Siegelbaum, and A. J. Hudspeth (New York: McGraw-Hill Professional, 2012), 602–620.

[8]D. G. Pelli, "Uncertainty Explains Many Aspects of Visual Contrast Detection and Discrimination" *Journal of the Optical Society of America* A2(9): 1508–32 (1985). D. G. Pelli, "The Quantum Efficiency of Vision," in *Vision: Coding and Efficiency*, ed. C. Blakemore (Cambridge: Cambridge University Press, 1990), 3–24. G. Sperling, "The Information Available in Brief Visual Presentations," *Psychological Monographs: General and Applied* 74(11, Whole No. 498): 1–29 (1960).

ence can accurately reflect the properties of the external world.[9] At the extreme, short viewing times and low levels of illumination simply reduce the number of correlated photons reaching the retina to the point where they scarcely exceed photon noise, and uncertainty is very high.[10] At slightly longer viewing times and greater illumination levels, signal-to-noise levels improve, but there may remain marked limits on visual sensitivity. Visual acuity, for example, which is a measure of the ability to resolve the fine spatial details of a visual pattern, is known to decline significantly with decreases in illumination.[11]

Signal-to-noise loss can depend on the direction of the observer's gaze. Visual acuity is highest at the observer's center of gaze. The center is the part of your visual system that is used for fine sensing, such as reading or scrutinizing faces in a social context. Acuity drops off markedly with angular distance from this center, such that the quality and quantity of information sensed a mere 10 degrees from center are far less than what is available at the center of gaze.[12]

Under unrestricted viewing conditions, the movements of the eyes largely overcome the effects of gaze direction. However, under the viewing conditions associated with a typical crime, this source of noise may place severe limitations on the ability of the observer to sense key pieces of information that are not present at the center of gaze. To appreciate the impact of these limitations, consider that patients with macular degeneration are effectively blinded in the region of the visual field possessing highest acuity, and must rely instead on the much-reduced quality of visual information gained from the peripheral visual field. To compensate for this clinical loss, images and text must be greatly magnified to enable comprehension—an option that is clearly not available to an eyewitness.

Visual Attention

Light falling on all parts of the retina is available to be sensed—and *must* be sensed for it to be available for further processing—but only a

[9]G. Sperling, "A Signal-to-Noise Theory of the Effects of Luminance on Picture Memory: Comment on Loftus," *Journal of Experimental Psychology: General* 115(2): 189–192 (1986).

[10]S. Hecht, S. Schlaer, and M. H. Pirenne, "Energy, Quanta, and Vision," *Journal of General Physiology* 25(6): 819–840 (1942).

[11]P. W. Cobb, "The Influence of Illumination of the Eye on Visual Acuity," *American Journal of Physiology* 29: 76–99 (1911). S. Hecht, "A Quantitative Basis for the Relation Between Visual Acuity and Illumination," *Proceedings of the National Academy of Sciences* 13: 569–574 (1927). S. Shlaer, "The Relation Between Visual Acuity and Illumination," *Journal of General Physiology* 21 (2): 165–188 (1937).

[12]H. Strasburger, I. Rentschler, and M. Jüttner, "Peripheral Vision and Pattern Recognition: A Review," *Journal of Vision* 11(5):13, 1–82 (2011).

small fraction of the information sensed reaches awareness or is used by the observer for recognition, action, or storage in memory. This limited access to visual sensory information is a product of selective attention.[13] Attention is an active process that can be directed by external factors—visual attributes with high salience, such as a bright light or an unfamiliar object—or by internal control.[14] If you are searching for a coffee cup, for example, you may explicitly direct your attention to the table where it was last seen. Attention can be directed to different types of image content, including specific locations in space,[15] specific image features (such as a specific color),[16] or to specific objects (such as the coffee cup).[17]

Attended image content is transiently enhanced to increase the fidelity of visual experience.[18] Attention interacts with sensory processing, for example, by selectively enhancing contrast[19] and potentially overcoming low signal-to-noise levels resulting from limited viewing time or illumination.[20] The effects of attention on contrast enhancement can be potentiated further when attention is commanded by emotionally laden stimuli.[21] Image con-

---

[13]W. James, *Principles of Psychology* (New York: Henry Holt, 1890); H. Pashler, J. Johnston, and E. Ruthruff, "Attention and Performance," *Annual Review of Psychology* 52: 629–651 (2001).

[14]M. I. Posner, "Orienting of Attention," *Quarterly Journal of Experimental Psychology* 32: 3–25 (1980).

[15]Ibid.

[16]A. F. Rossi and M. A. Paradiso, "Feature-specific Effects of Selective Visual Attention," *Vision Research* 35(5): 621–634 (1995).

[17]J. Duncan, "Selective Attention and the Organization of Visual Information," *Journal of Experimental Psychology: General* 113(4): 501–517 (1984).

[18]H. Pashler, J. Johnston, and E. Ruthruff, "Attention and Performance," *Annual Review of Psychology* 52: 629–651 (2001).

[19]M. Carrasco et al.,"Attention Alters Appearance" *Nature Neuroscience* 7: 308–313 (2004).

[20]M. I. Posner, C. R. Snyder, and B. J. Davidson, "Attention and the Detection of Signals," *Journal of Experimental Psychology* 109(2): 160–174 (1980). M. Carrasco and B. McElree, "Covert Attention Accelerates the Rate of Visual Information Processing," *Proceedings of the National Academies of Science* 98(9): 5363–5367 (2001). Y. Yeshurun and M. Carrasco, "Attention Improves or Impairs Visual Performance by Enhancing Spatial Resolution," *Nature* 396, 72–75 (1998). M. Carrasco et al., "Covert Attention Increases Spatial Resolution with or without Masks: Support for Signal Enhancement," *Journal of Vision* 2(6): 467–79 (2002). E. Blaser et al., "Measuring the Amplification of Attention," *Proceedings of the National Academies of Science* 96(20): 11681–11686 (1999). K. Anton-Erxleben and M. Carrasco, "Attentional Enhancement of Spatial Resolution: Linking Behavioural and Neurophysiological Evidence," *Nature Reviews Neuroscience* 14(3):188–200 (2013). J. W. Couperus and G. R. Mangun, "Signal Enhancement and Suppression During Visual-Spatial Selective Attention," *Brain Research* 1359:155–177 (2010).

[21]E. A. Phelps, S. Ling, and M. Carrasco, "Emotion Facilitates Perception and Potentiates: The Perceptual Benefits of Attention," *Psychological Science* 17(4): 292 (2006).

tent *not* falling within the focus of attention is processed with less fidelity.[22] In some cases, unattended content is effectively invisible: It does not reach awareness, it is not perceived, and it is not available for use in guiding decisions or actions, or for storage in memory.[23]

Different pieces of visual information compete for selection,[24] as their attributes of physical salience, location in space, novelty, and relevance to the observer's needs and behavioral goals are always changing.[25] The outcome of the competition is highly susceptible to noise (in this instance, noise is defined as uncontrolled factors that bias the focus of attention and create uncertainty about the content of a visual scene), because the informational content of the visual image vastly exceeds what can be attended at any point in time. The implications of such noise for eyewitness identification are profound. An observer must "select" what to attend to, often within a short window of time, without advance warning, in the presence of many novel objects and events, and under such confounding influences as anxiety and fear.

The signal detection framework is readily adaptable to the problem of noise in visual attention and provides some insights into the limits of attentional selection in the presence of noise.[26] In essence, this signal detection approach quantifies the extent to which multiple items competing with one another for attention affect attentional enhancement for any one of the items.[27] Reductions in efficiency are common under such noise conditions. Indeed, sensitivity to unattended items can be markedly reduced under conditions of high "perceptual load," in which there are many objects si-

---

[22]Posner, Snyder, and Davidson, "Attention and the Detection of Signals." Y. Yeshurun and M Carrasco, "Attention Improves or Impairs Visual Performance by Enhancing Spatial Resolution," *Nature* 396: 72–75 (November 1998).

[23]A. Mack and I. Rock, *Inattentional Blindness* (Cambridge, MA: MIT Press, 1998).

[24]R. Desimone and J. Duncan, "Neural Mechanism of Selective Visual Attention," *Annual Review of Neuroscience* 18: 193–222 (March 1995).

[25]J. M. Wolfe and T. S. Horowitz, "What Attributes Guide the Deployment of Visual Attention and How Do They Do It?" *Nature Reviews Neuroscience* 5: 495–501 (June 2004). H. E. Egeth and S.Yantis, "Visual Attention: Control, Representation, and Time Course," *Annual Review of Psychology* 48(1): 269–297 (February 1997). M. I. Posner, "Orienting in Attention," *Quarterly Journal of Experimental Psychology* 32(1): 3–25 (1980). A. Treisman and G. Gelade, "A Feature Integration Theory of Attention," *Cognitive Psychology* 12(1):97–136 (January 1980). L. Itti and C. Koch, "A Saliency-based Search Mechanism for Overt and Covert Shifts of Visual Attention," *Vision Research* 40(10–12): 1489–1506 (June 2000).

[26]G. Sperling and M. J. Melchner, "The Attention Operating Characteristic: Examples from Visual Search," *Science* 202(4365): 315–318 (October 1978). G. Sperling and B. A. Dosher, "Strategy and Optimization in Human Information Processing," in *Handbook of Perception and Human Performance*, ed. K. Boff, L. Kaufman, and J. Thomas (New York: Wiley, 1986).

[27]Ibid.

multaneously competing for attention.[28] The spacing of items in the visual field also impacts visual sensitivity.[29] When objects are closely spaced, their discriminability is reduced. One explanation offered for this "crowding effect" is that the spacing of visual items is smaller than the resolution of visual attention.[30] The visual phenomenon of crowding suggests that a crime committed in a visually complex scene, such as a sporting event, could easily place limits on the ability of a witness to accurately perceive the facial features of a perpetrator.

A related consequence of attentional noise is that competing interests can readily hijack the attentional focus. The technique of *misdirection*— one of the original mainstays of performance magic—directs attention to uninformative image content and exploits the invisibility of unattended features.[31] The well-studied *inattentional blindness* effect is another example of this phenomenon, in which attention that is pre-directed to one behaviorally significant property of a visual scene precludes awareness of other features that also may be important.[32] (For a dramatic demonstration of this effect, produced by Simons and Chabris,[33] see http://tinyurl.com/inattentional-blindness.)

Inattentional blindness effects translate well to real-world interactions between people. An individual can be surprisingly unaware of surreptitious changes to the physical appearance of another person while engaged in conversation.[34] One demonstration of this phenomenon involved two strangers (experimenter and pedestrian) in a brief face-to-face conversation on a sidewalk. At some point in the conversation an opaque door was carried between the two individuals, and another person with different appearance, clothing, and voice quickly replaced the experimenter. More than half of

---

[28]N. Lavie, "Perceptual Load as a Necessary Condition for Selective Attention," *Journal of Experimental Psychology: Human Perception and Performance* 21(3): 451–468 (June 1995). J. W. Couperus, "Perceptual Load Influences Selective Attention Across Development," *Developmental Psychology* 47(5):1431–1439 (September 2011).

[29]D. M. Levi, "Crowding—An Essential Bottleneck for Object Recognition: A Mini-review," *Vision Research* 48: 635–654 (2008).

[30]J. Intriligator and P. Cavanagh, "The Spatial Resolution of Visual Attention," *Cognitive Psychology* 43: 171–216 (2001).

[31]G. Kuhn et al., "Misdirection in Magic: Implications for the Relationship Between Eye Gaze and Attention," *Visual Cognition* 16(2–3): 391–405 (2008). S. L. Macknik, S. Martinez-Conde, and S. Blakeslee, *Sleights of Mind: What the Neuroscience of Magic Reveals About Our Everyday Deceptions* (New York: Henry Holt and Co., 2010).

[32]A. Mack and I. Rock, *Inattentional Blindness* (Cambridge, MA: MIT Press, 1998). U. Neisser and R. Becklen, "Selective Looking: Attending to Visually Specified Events," *Cognitive Psychology* 7(4): 480–494 (October 1975). D. Simons, "Attentional Capture and Inattentional Blindness," *Trends in Cognitive Sciences* 4(4): 147–155 (April 2000).

[33]D. J. Simons and C. F. Chabris, "Gorillas in Our Midst: Sustained Inattentional Blindness for Dynamic Events," *Perception* 28: 1059–1074 (1999).

[34]D. J. Simons and D. T. Levin, "Failure to Detect Changes to People During a Real-World Interaction," *Psychonomic Bulletin and Review* 5(4): 644–649 (1998).

the participants (pedestrians) failed to notice that their conversation partner had changed. This finding suggests that naturally occurring events that briefly divert attention have the potential to markedly impair the accuracy of eyewitness identifications.

Attentional hijacking is particularly characteristic of stimuli that elicit strong emotional responses, such as fear and arousal.[35] Visual stimuli that trigger fear responses act as powerful external cues that command attention.[36] While this potentiates sensitivity to those stimuli, at the considerable expense of sensitivity to others, it is often the case that the attended emotional stimuli are not the ones with relevant informational content.[37]The so-called weapon focus is a real-world case in point for eyewitness identification, in which attention is compellingly drawn to emotionally laden stimuli, such as a gun or a knife, at the expense of acquiring greater visual information about the face of the perpetrator (see also discussion of weapon focus in Chapter 5).[38] (One might argue that this is an adaptation that benefits immediate action or engagement with a threatening stimulus, but is surely detrimental to one's efforts to bear witness.)

Visual Perception

Visual perception is the conscious functional result of efforts to identify the environmental causes of the pattern of light cast onto the back of the eye.[39] Perception does not reflect the sensory world passively, as camera film detects patterns of light. On the contrary, visual perception is constructive

---

[35]C. H. Hansen and R. D. Hansen, "Finding the Face in the Crowd: An Anger Superiority Effect," *Journal of Personality and Social Psychology* 54: 917–924 (1988). E. Fox et al., "Facial Expressions of Emotion: Are Angry Faces Detected More Efficiently?" *Cognition and Emotion* 14(1): 61–92 (2000). R. Compton, "The Interface Between Emotion and Attention: A Review of Evidence from Psychology and Neuroscience," *Behavioral and Cognitive Neuroscience Reviews* 2(2): 115–129 (2003). R. L. Bannerman, E. V. Temminck, and A. Sahraie, "Emotional Stimuli Capture Spatial Attention But Do Not Modulate Spatial Memory," *Vision Research* 65: 12–20 (15 July 2012).

[36]J. A. Easterbrook, "The Effects of Emotion on Cue Utilization and the Organization of Behavior," *Psychological Review* 66(3): 183–201 (1959).

[37]E. Ferneyhough et al., "Anxiety Modulates the Effects of Emotion and Attention on Early Vision," *Cognition and Emotion* 27(1): 166–176 (2013). G. Pourtois and P. Vuilleumier, "Dynamics of Emotional Effects on Spatial Attention in the Human Visual Cortex," *Progress in Brain Research* 156: 67–91 (2006).

[38]T. Kramer, R. Buckhout, and P. Eugenio, "Weapon Focus, Arousal, and Eyewitness Memory: Attention Must Be Paid," *Law and Human Behavior* 14(2): 167–184 (1990). R. S. Truelove, "Do Weapons Automatically Capture Attention," *Applied Cognitive Psychology* 20(7): 871–893 (2006). E. F. Loftus, G. R. Loftus, and J. Messo, "Some Facts About 'Weapon Focus'," *Law and Human Behavior* 11(1): 55–62 (1987).

[39]W. James, *Principles of Psychology* (New York: Henry Holt, 1890). S. Harnad, ed., *Categorical Perception: The Groundwork of Cognition* (New York: Cambridge University Press, 1987). T. D. Albright, "Perceiving," *Daedalus* (in press).

and entails (1) integrating and segmenting attended attributes of the visual image into objects, (2) complementing and interpreting the product with expectations derived from memory of prior experiences with the world, and (3) assigning meaning and emotional valence by reference to prior knowledge of function and value.[40] All of these perceptual processes are affected by noise. Because the things perceived are the things we place into memory, perceptual noise can dramatically limit the accuracy of eyewitness identification.

The process of feature integration and interpretation may be distorted by images of an object unique to a specific angle of view.[41] The retinal pattern generated by a face viewed directly from the front differs considerably—with changes in aspect ratio and relative placement of facial features—from that generated by a face viewed from an oblique side angle. Viewing a face from an angle above or below center (as might be the case if the criminal were standing over you, or below you on the stairs) also yields retinal distortions of facial features. In this case, the distortions prominently mimick facial gestures of smiling versus frowning, and perhaps cause incorrect inferences about the emotional state of the person observed and his or her intentions and motivations. (This distortion is the basis for the Japanese Noh Theatre mask effect, in which a rigid mask tilted forward leads to the appearance of a smile and backward leads to the appearance of a frown—an effect you can simulate by simply looking into the mirror and tilting your face up or down.)[42]

Viewing conditions can also affect the perception of face, gender, and age.[43] Investigators found that faces that were physically identical—and particularly those bordering on androgyny—were perceived as unambiguously male or female depending on where they appeared in the observer's visual field. The spatial patterning of these effects was distinctive and stable for each observer. Perceptual distortions of this sort are a source of noise that may have important implications for the accuracy of eyewitness identification.

Perceptual distortions also may be introduced through memory recall.

---

[40]C. D. Gilbert, "The Constructive Nature of Visual Processing," in *Principles of Neuroscience*, 5th Edition, ed. E. Kandel, J. H. Schwartz, T. M. Jessell, S. A. Siegelbaum, and A. J. Hudspeth (New York: McGraw-Hill Professional, 2012). T. D. Albright, "On the Perception of Probable Things: Neural Substrates of Associative Memory, Imagery, and Perception," *Neuron* 74 (2): 227–245 (2012).

[41]W. G. Hayward and P. Williams, "Viewpoint Dependence and Object Discriminability," *Psychological Science* 11(1): 7–12 (2000).

[42]M. J. Lyons et al., "The Noh Mask Effect: Vertical Viewpoint Dependence on Facial Expression Perception," *Proceedings of the Royal Society B: Biological Sciences* 267(1459): 2239–2245 (2000).

[43]A. Afraz, M. Vaziri-Pashkam, and P. Cavanagh, "Spatial Heterogeneity in the Perception of Face and Form Attributes," *Current Biology* 20(23): 2112–2116 (2010).

The way an observer experiences a visual scene—the setting, the people, and the actions associated with a crime —is commonly influenced as much by expectations from prior experience with the world as it is by the precise patterns of light cast upon the retina. There are good reasons why this is true. As noted above, the sensory input (the pattern of light received) is often noisy, incomplete, and ambiguous, and memories of what is *likely* to be out there, given the context, are called on to fill in the blanks, reconcile ambiguities, and leave clear and coherent percepts.[44] This perceptual completion is probabilistic.[45] It is an hypothesis, and the accuracy naturally depends on the degree to which the observer's expectations match the noisy sensory data.

What is implied is that the same mechanism that grants the certainty of perceptual experience in the face of noise and ambiguity is also capable of implicitly fabricating content that does not correspond to external reality and yet is experienced with no less certainty. Performance magic relies on this constructive nature of perceptual experience, and that nature is also the foundation for many visual illusions and forms of visual art.[46] In a classic experiment that drives home the point, Bruner and Postman looked at the ability of observers to recognize "trick" playing cards.[47] The trick cards were created by altering the color of a given suit (e.g., a red seven of spades). Observers were shown a series of cards with brief presentations. Some cards were trick, and the remainder normal. With astonishing frequency, observers reported that the trick cards were normal. When questioned, observers defended their reports, even after being allowed to scrutinize the trick cards, thus demonstrating that learned properties of the world are capable of sharply altering our experience and, moreover, reinforcing our convictions about what we have seen, even in the face of countermanding sensory evidence. In view of this inherent dependence of perception on prior experiences and context—and, importantly, the fact that the viewer is commonly none the wiser when perception differs from

---

[44]Albright, "On the Perception of Probable Things."

[45]D. C. Knill and W. Richards, *Perception as Bayesian Inference*, ed. D. C. Knill and W. Richards (Cambridge: Cambridge University Press, 1996). D. Kersten "High-level Vision as Statistical Inference," in *The New Cognitive Neurosciences*, 2nd Edition, ed. M. S. Gazzaniga (Cambridge: MIT Press, 1999), 353–363. D. Kersten, P. Mamassian, and A. Yuille, "Object Perception as Bayesian Inference," *Annual Review of Psychology* 55: 271–304 (February 2004).

[46]E. H. Gombrich, *Art and Illusion. A Study in the Psychology of Pictorial Representation* (London: Phaidon 1960). T. D. Albright, "The Veiled Christ of Cappella Sansevero: On Art, Vision and Reality," *Leonardo* 46(1): 19–23 (2013). Macknik, Martinez-Conde, and Blakeslee, *Sleights of Mind: What the Neuroscience of Magic Reveals About Our Everyday Deceptions* (New York: Henry Holt and Co., 2010).

[47]J. S. Bruner and L. Postman, "On the Perception of Incongruity: A Paradigm," *Journal of Personality* 18(2): 206–223 (1949).

the "ground truth" of the external world—it appears that accurate eyewitness identification may be difficult to achieve.

Additional noise (in this case defined as uncertainty resulting from loss of perceptual resolution) may result from the fact that visual perception is categorical.[48] Although the objects of our experience vary broadly along multiple sensory dimensions, we lump them into categories based upon prior associations, many of which stem from common functions, physical properties, meanings, or emotional valence. Apples in a basket or the many typographic fonts for the letter "A" are visually distinct, yet we readily perceive them as categorically identical. For most behavioral and cognitive goals, perceptual processing is greatly simplified by treating all members of a category as the same, despite their differences. It rarely matters, for example, whether the apple we choose is dappled on one side or irregular in shape, nor does the font used bear greatly on our ability to read. One of the functional corollaries of categorical perception is that observers are far better at discriminating between objects from different categories than objects from the same category.[49] Evidence indicates that the structure of object memory is also categorical, suggesting that perceived objects are encoded in memory as a category type, often without specific detail.[50]

Perceptual categorization naturally applies to faces.[51] We readily categorize faces by distinctions along the obvious dimensions of gender, age,

[48]W. James, *Principles of Psychology* (New York: Henry Holt, 1980). S. Harnad, ed., *Categorical Perception: The Groundwork of Cognition* (New York: Cambridge University Press, 1987).

[49]R. Goldstone, "Influences of Categorization on Perceptual Discrimination," *Journal of Experimental Psychology General* 123(2): 178–200 (1994). R. Goldstone, Y. Lippa, and R. M. Shiffrin, "Altering Object Representations Through Category Learning," *Cognition* 78(1): 27–43 (2001).

[50]E. Tulving, "Episodic and Semantic Memory," in *Organization of Memory*, ed. E. Tulving and W. Donaldson (New York: Academic Press, 1972), 381–403. L. K. Tyler et al., "Processing Objects at Different Levels of Specificity," *Journal of Cognitive Neuroscience* 16(3): 351–362 (2004). M. J. Farah and J. L. McClelland, "A Computational Model of Semantic Memory Impairment: Modality Specificity and Emergent Category Specificity," *Journal of Experimental Psychology: General* 120 (4): 339–357 (1991). C. Gerlach et al., "Categorization and Category Effects in Normal Object Recognition: A PET Study," *Neuropsychologia* 38(13): 1693–1703 (2000). G. W. Humphreys and E. M. Forde, "Hierarchies, Similarity, and Interactivity in Object Recognition: 'Category-Specific' Neuropsychological Deficits," *Behavioral and Brain Sciences* 24(3): 453–476 (2001).

[51]J. M. Beale and F. C. Keil, "Categorical Effects in the Perception of Faces," *Cognition* 57(3): 217–239 (1995). D. T. Levin, "Classifying Faces by Race: The Structure of Face Categories," *Journal of Experimental Psychology: Learning, Memory, and Cognition* 22(6):1364–1382 (1996). D. T. Levin and J. Beale, "Categorical Perception Occurs in Newly Learned Faces, Cross-Race Faces, and Inverted Faces," *Perception and Psychophysics* 62: 386–401 (2000). M. A. Webster et al., "Adaptation to Natural Facial Categories," *Nature* 428(6982): 557–561 (2004). Y. Lee et al., "Broadly Tuned Face Representation in Older Adults Assessed by Categorical Perception,"*Journal of Experimental Psychology: Human Perception and Performance* 40(3): 1060–1071 (2014).

and race, but we also draw distinctions along dimensions such as skin tone, hair color and style, presence and type of facial hair, such subtler factors as shape of cheeks and jaw, and subjective qualities such as attractiveness. The practical consequence of this for eyewitness identification is that the precision of a perceptual experience may be reduced within any of these categories, particularly because we typically witness criminal events for such a brief period of time. The ensuing memory of the experience will likely reflect that reduced precision, and the memory retrieved may regress to a category prototype or to other exemplars of the perceived category.[52] The witness may categorically perceive a square jawed man with a moustache, but the fine details needed for individuation of a suspect are neither perceived nor encoded in memory. For example, although you may have seen the iconic Marlboro Man countless times on billboards and in magazines, it is unlikely that you could distinguish him in a lineup from other square jawed mustachioed men.

MEMORY

Functional Processes of Memory

Conscious visual perceptual experiences, rendered by the processes described in the previous section on vision, are commonly stored as *declarative memories*, meaning that they can be consciously accessed and expressed as knowledge about the world (as distinct from *procedural memories*, such as motor skills).[53] Declarative memories are of two types, semantic and episodic, reflecting a distinction between memories of meanings, facts, and concepts versus memories of events (such as those witnessed during a crime).[54] Declarative memories are conceptualized as involving three core processes—encoding, storage, and retrieval—which refer to the placement of items in memory, their maintenance therein, and subsequent access to the stored information.[55]

Like vision, memory is also beset by noise. Encoding, storage, and remembering are not passive, static processes that record, retain, and divulge

---

[52] J. Huttenlocher, L. V. Hedges, and J. L. Vevea, "Why Do Categories Affect Stimulus Judgement?" *Journal of Experimental Psychology: General* 129(2): 220–241 (2000). R. Goldstone, Y. Lippa, and R. M. Shiffrin, "Altering Object Representations Through Category Learning," *Cognition* 78(1): 27–43 (2001).

[53] W. James, *Principles of Psychology* (New York: Henry Holt, 1890). B. Milner, *Physiologie de l'hippocampe*, ed. P. Passouant (Paris: Centre National de la Recherche Scientifique, 1962), 257–272. L. R. Squire and J. Wixted, "The Cognitive Neuroscience of Human Memory since H.M.," *Annual Review of Neuroscience* 34: 259–288 (2011).

[54] Tulving, "Episodic and Semantic Memory."

[55] E. Tulving, "Organization of Memory: Quo vadis?" in *The Cognitive Neurosciences*, ed. M. S. Gazzaniga (Cambridge, MA: MIT Press, 1995), 839–847.

their contents in an informational vacuum, unaffected by outside influences. The contents cannot be treated as a veridical permanent record, like photographs stored in a safe. On the contrary, the fidelity of our memories for real events may be compromised by many factors at all stages of processing, from encoding through storage, to the final stages of retrieval. Without awareness, we regularly encode events in a biased manner and subsequently forget, reconstruct, update, and distort the things we believe to be true.[56]

The following sections discuss memory encoding, storage, and retrieval, with emphasis on the limits of these processes as they pertain to eyewitness identification. Emotions can strongly influence these processes of memory; some specific actions are highlighted. The phenomenon of "recognition memory" is also discussed. This refers to the specific type of memory retrieval in which a stimulus (e.g., a face) is used to probe memory, and the rememberer (e.g., an eyewitness) must decide whether the strength of the elicited memory evidence is sufficient to declare that the stimulus was previously encountered or is novel. Recognition memory underlies eyewitness identification, as the witness must make a recognition decision.

Memory Encoding

Memory encoding refers to the process whereby perceived objects and events are initially placed into storage. The encoding process involves two stages, which are commonly distinguished by the quantity of information stored, the duration of storage, and the susceptibility to interference.[57] Short-term or working memory is the conscious content of recent perceptual experiences or information recently recalled from long-term storage. Information that remains at the focus of attention persists in and forms the contents of short-term memory. This form of memory is of limited duration

---

[56]J. T. Wixted, "The Psychology and Neuroscience of Forgetting," *Annual Review of Psychology* 55: 235–269 (2004). E. Tulving and D. M. Thomson, "Encoding Specificity and Retrieval Processes in Episodic Memory," *Psychological Review* 80(5): 352–373 (1973). Y. Dudai, "Reconsolidation: The Advantage of Being Refocused," *Current Opinion in Neurobiology* 16(2): 174–178 (2006). E. F. Loftus, "Planting Misinformation in the Human Mind: A 30-Year Investigation of the Malleability of Memory," *Learning and Memory* 12(4): 361–366 (2005). R. A. Bjork, "Interference and Memory," in *Encyclopedia of Learning and Memory*, ed. L. R. Squire (New York: Macmillan, 1992), 283–288. J. A. McGeoch, "Forgetting and the Law of Disuse," *Psychological Review* 39(4): 352–370 (1932). J. G. Jenkins and K. M. Dallenbach, "Obliviscence during Sleep and Waking," *The American Journal of Psychology* 35(4): 605–612 (1924). B. J. Underwood and L. Postman, "Extra-Experimental Sources of Interference in Forgetting," *Psychological Review* 67 (2): 73–95 (1960).

[57]R. C. Atkinson and R. M. Shiffrin, "Human Memory: A Proposed System and its Control Processes," in *The Psychology of Learning and Motivation* (Volume 2), ed. K. W. Spence and J. T. Spence (New York: Academic Press,1968), 89–195. W. James, *Principles of Psychology* (New York: Henry Holt, 1890). A. Baddeley, "Working Memory: Looking Back and Looking Forward," *Nature Reviews Neuroscience* 4(10): 829–839 (2003). A. Baddley, *Working Memory* (New York: Oxford University Press, 1986).

and capacity[58] and labile, decaying quickly with time and easily disrupted by other perceptual or cognitive processes.[59] Through cellular and molecular events that play out over time, the contents of short-term memories may be encoded and consolidated into long-term memory,[60] which is more enduring (albeit evolving with ongoing experience), and of greater capacity.

The structure of an individual's full library of long-term declarative memories can be thought of as a collection of associations between items of specific semantic (e.g., the fact that that person X is a 34-year-old female) or episodic content (e.g., the fact that person X was at location Y on the night of the witnessed crime).[61] As the individual gains new experiences, long-term declarative memories may be updated by adding new content to the existing library or by forming new associations between existing content.[62]

Memories are particularly labile during the encoding process. The contents of short-term memory are limited and highly subject to interference by subsequent sensory, cognitive, emotional, or behavioral events; the contents can also be biased by prior knowledge, expectations, or beliefs, resulting in a distorted representation of experience. Short-term memories of events that happened early in a witnessed proceeding may simply be forgotten with the passage of time or badly compromised by attention directed to subsequent emotional events or cognitive and behavioral demands (e.g., anxiety, fear, the need to escape). In such cases, the compromised information may never be consolidated fully into long-term storage or that storage may contain distorted content.[63] At the same time, the quality of encoding of stimuli that are attended is commonly enhanced by highly emotional content.[64]

---

[58]G. A. Miller, "The Magical Number Seven," *The Psychological Review* 63(2): 81–97 (1956).

[59]J. Jonides et al., "The Mind and Brain of Short-Term Memory," *Annual Review of Psychology* 59: 193–224 (2008).

[60]E. Kandel and L. Squire, *Memory: From Mind to Molecules* (New York: Scientific American Library, 2008).

[61]J. R. Anderson, *The Architecture of Cognition* (Cambridge: Harvard University Press, 1983). J. R. Anderson and C. Lebiere, *The Atomic Components of Thought* (Mahwah: Lawrence Erlbaum Associates, 1998).

[62]M. P. Walker et al., "Dissociable Stages of Human Memory Consolidation and Reconsolidation," *Nature* 425: 616 (2003).

[63]J. L. McGaugh, "Memory—a Century of Consolidation," *Science* 287(5451): 248–251 (2000). J. L. McGaugh and B. Roozendaal, "Role of Adrenal Stress Hormones in Forming Lasting Memories in the Brain," *Current Opinion in Neurobiology* 12(2): 205–210 (2002).

[64]K. N. Ochsner, "Are Affective Events Richly Recollected or Simply Familiar? The Experience and Process of Recognizing Feelings Past," *Journal of Experimental Psychology: General* 129 (2): 242–261 (2000). D. Talmi, et al., "Immediate Memory Consequences of the Effect of Emotion on Attention to Pictures," *Learning and Memory* 15(2008): 172–182. E. A. Kensinger and D. L. Schacter, "Neural Processes Supporting Young and Older Adults' Emotional Memories," *Journal of Cognitive Neuroscience* 7 (2008): 1–13. E. A. Phelps. "Emotion and Cognition: Insights from Studies of the Human Amygdala," *Annual Review of Psychology* 57: 27–53 (2006).

Memory Storage

Memory storage refers to the long-term retention of information after encoding. The stability of stored information is continuously challenged and subject to modification. We forget, qualify, or distort existing memories as we acquire new perceptual experiences and encode new content and associations into memory.[65]

Forgetting can be partially mitigated, and memories stabilized, by habits of retrieval (or reactivation) and reconsolidation, which happen whenever we tell the story of our experiences.[66] Reactivation is not perfect. With each implicit retrieval or explicit telling of a story, we may unconsciously smooth over inconsistencies or modify content based on our prior beliefs, the accounts of others, or through the lens of new information. We may add embellishments that reflect opinions, emotions, or prejudices[67] rather than observed facts; or we may simply omit disturbing content and pass over fine details.[68]

A second threat to the stability of long-term memories is, ironically, our life-long ability to learn new things. Because memory mechanisms are inherently plastic throughout life, content stored for the long term is surprisingly labile in the face of new information. Our memories are thus an ever-evolving account of our experiences. A memory that reflects witnessing person X at location Y on a particular evening might be readily and notably updated by subsequent learning that location Y is the home of a business associate of person X. Our memories of the witnessed actions of person

---

[65]J. T. Wixted, "The Psychology and Neuroscience of Forgetting," *Annual Review of Psychology* 55: 235–269 (2004). Tulving and Thomson, "Encoding Specificity and Retrieval Processes." Y. Dudai, "Reconsolidation: The Advantage of Being Refocused," *Current Opinion in Neurobiology* 16(2): 174–178 (2006). E. F. Loftus, "Planting Misinformation in the Human Mind: A 30-Year Investigation of the Malleability of Memory," *Learning and Memory* 12(4): 361–366 (2005). R. A. Bjork, "Interference and Memory," in *Encyclopedia of Learning and Memory*, ed. L. R. Squire (New York: Macmillan, 1992), 283–288. J. A. McGeoch, "Forgetting and the Law of Disuse," *Psychological Review* 39(4): 352–370 (1932). J. G. Jenkins and K. M. Dallenbach, "Obliviscence During Sleep and Waking," *The American Journal of Psychology* 35 (1924): 605–612. B. J. Underwood and L. Postman, "Extra-Experimental Sources of Interference in Forgetting," *Psychological Review* 67(2): 73–95 (1960). E. F. Loftus, "The Malleability of Human Memory," *American Scientist* 67(3): 312–320 (1979). D. J. Yi et al., "When a Thought Equals a Look: Refreshing Enhances Perceptual Memory," *Journal of Cognitive Neuroscience* 20(8): 1371–1380 (2008).

[66]C. M. Alberini, *Memory Reconsolidation* (Waltham: Academic Press, 2013).

[67]D. L. Schacter, *Psychology*, Second Edition (New York: Worth Publishers, 2011), 253–254. E. F. Loftus and H. G. Hoffman, "Misinformation and Memory, the Creation of New Memories," *Journal of Experimental Psychology* 118(1): 100–104 (1989). G. Mazzoni and A. Memon, "Imagination Can Create False Autobiographical Memories," *Psychological Science* 14(2): 186–188 (2003).

[68]F. C. Bartlett, *Remembering: A Study in Experimental and Social Psychology* (London: Cambridge University Press, 1932).

X may be qualified by new knowledge of his or her life history. Moreover, because new content can be added and the source of that content forgotten, we may attribute our updated memories to the originally witnessed events—in some cases substantially changing what we believe we have seen.[69] It is thus not surprising that newly incorporated information need not be true to fact. Research on *false memories* shows that it is possible to plant fabricated content in memory, which leads us to recall things we never experienced.[70]

The emotional content of stored memories is a factor that appears to promote long-term retention; memories of highly arousing emotional stimuli, such as those associated with a witnessed crime, tend to be more enduring than memories of non-arousing stimuli.[71] Highly salient, unexpected, or arousing events—such as the Kennedy assassination or the Space Shuttle disaster—are commonly more strongly stored in memory, and their later retrieval is often associated with the subjective experience

---

[69]D. S. Lindsay and M. K. Johnson, "Recognition Memory and Source Monitoring," *Bulletin of the Psychonomic Society* 29(3): 203–205 (1991). D. L. Schacter and C. S. Dodson, "Misattribution, False Recognition and the Sins of Memory," *Philosophical Transactions of the Royal Society: Biological Sciences* 356(1413): 1385–1393 (2001). L. A. Henkel, N. Franklin, and M. K. Johnson, "Cross-Modal Source Monitoring Confusions Between Perceived and Imagined Events," *Journal of Experimental Psychology: Learning, Memory, and Cognition* 26(2): 321–335 (2000). D. L. Schacter, ed., *Memory Distortion: How Minds, Brains, and Societies Reconstruct the Past* (Cambridge, MA: Harvard University Press, 1995). K. J. Mitchell and M. K. Johnson, "Source Monitoring: Attributing Mental Experiences," in *The Oxford Handbook of Memory*, ed. E. Tulving and F. I. M. Craik (New York: Oxford University Press, 2000), 179–195. H. L. Roediger III and K. B. McDermott, "Creating False Memories: Remembering Words Not Presented in Lists," *Journal of Experimental Psychology: Learning, Memory, and Cognition* 21(4): 803–814 (1985).
[70]Loftus, "Planting Misinformation in the Human Mind." E. F. Loftus and J. E. Pickrell, "The Formation of False Memories," *Psychiatric Annals* 25(12): 720–725 (1995). M. K. Johnson and C. L. Raye, "False Memories and Confabulation," *Trends in Cognitive Sciences* 2(4): 137–145 (1998).
[71]L. J. Kleinsmith and S. Kaplan, "Paired-Associate Learning as a Function of Arousal and Interpolated Interval" *Journal of Experimental Psychology* 65(2): 190–193 (1963). M. W. Eysenck, "Arousal, Learning, and Memory," *Psychological Bulletin* 83(3): 389–404 (1976). F. Heuer and D. Reisberg, "Vivid Memories of Emotional Events: The Accuracy of Remembered Minutiae," *Memory and Cognition* 18(5): 496–450 (1990). T. Sharot and E. A. Phelps, "How Arousal Modulates Memory: Disentangling the Effects of Attention and Retention," *Cognitive, Affective, and Behavioral Neuroscience* 4(3): 294–306 (2004). E. A. Kensinger, R. J. Garoff-Eaton, and D. L. Schacter, "Memory for Specific Visual Details Can Be Enhanced by Negative Arousing Content," *Journal of Memory and Language* 54(1): 99–112 (2006). E. Kensinger, "Remembering Emotional Experiences: The Contribution of Valence and Arousal," *Reviews in the Neurosciences* 15(4): 241–251 (2004).

of high vivdness and a sense of reliving[72] (although not necessarily with greater accuracy, as detailed below). The stronger encoding and storage of emotional memories results from the engagement of a specialized system of stress hormones (glucocorticoids) which is triggered by arousing content and has potentiating effects on the neuronal processes underlying memory consolidation and storage.[73] Despite the vividness and the sense of reliving that characterizes retrieval of emotional memories, there are many indications that such memories are just as prone to errors.[74] This may reflect, in part, memory enhancements, of the sort described above, which accompany frequent re-consolidation or re-telling of the story of the emotional experience, and often include details (some true to fact, some not) learned after the experience.[75] Although emotional memories are often inaccurate in detail, one important corollary of their vividness is that they are frequently

[72]G. Wolters and J. J. Goudsmit, "Flashbulb and Event Memory of September 11, 2001: Consistency, Confidence and Age Effect," *Psychological Report* 96: 605–619 (2005). E. A. Kensinger, A. C. Krendl, and S. Corkin, "Memories of an Emotional and a Nonemotional Event: Effects of Aging and Delay Interval," *Experimental Aging Research* 32: 23–45 (2006). U. Neisser and N. Harsch, "Phantom Flashbulbs: False Recollections of Hearing the News about Challenger," in *Affect and Accuracy in Recall: Studies of "Flashbulb" Memories*, ed. E. Winograd and U. Neisser (New York: Cambridge University Press, 1992): 9–31. K. S. LaBar and E. A. Phelps, "Arousal-Mediated Memory Consolidation: Role of the Medial Temporal Lobe in Humans," *Psychological Science* 9(6): 490–493 (1998).

[73]J. L. McGaugh, "Memory: A Century of Consolidation," *Science* 287(5451): 248–251 (2000). J. L. McGaugh and B. Roozendaal, "Role of Adrenal Stress Hormones in Forming Lasting Memories in the Brain," *Current Opinion in Neurobiology* 12(2): 205–210 (2002).

[74]E. A. Kensinger, "Remembering the Details: Effects of Emotion," *Emotion Review* 1(2): 99–113 (2009). T. Sharot, M. R. Delgado, and E. A. Phelps, "How Emotion Enhances the Feeling of Remembering," *Nature Neuroscience* 7(12): 1376–1380 (2004). H. Schmolck, E. A. Buffalo, and L. R. Squire, "Memory Distortions Develop over Time: Recollections of the O. J. Simpson Trial Verdict after 15 And 32 Months," *Psychological Science* 11 (1): 39–45 (2000). S. R. Schmidt, "Autobiographical Memories for the September 11th Attacks: Reconstructive Errors and Emotional Impairment of Memory," *Memory and Cognition* 32(3): 443–454 (2004). T. W. Buchanan and R. Adolphs, "The Role of the Human Amygdala in Emotional Modulation of Long-Term Declarative Memory," in *Emotional Cognition: From Brain to Behavior*, ed. S. Moore and M. Oaksford (Amsterdam: John Benjamins Publishing, 2002), 9–34.

[75]E. Soleti et al., "Does Talking About Emotions Influence Eyewitness Memory? The Role of Emotional vs. Factual Retelling on Memory Accuracy," *Europe's Journal of Psychology* 8(4): 632–640 (2012).

held with high confidence.[76] This breakdown of the relationship between accuracy and confidence can obviously undermine eyewitness accounts.[77]

The enduring plasticity of stored memories is a serious concern for the validity of eyewitness identification. A witness' inevitable interactions with law enforcement and legal counsel, not to mention communications from journalists, family, and friends, have the potential to significantly modify the witness' memory of faces encountered and of other event details at the scene of the crime.[78] Thus, the fidelity of retrieved events—and the accuracy of identification—is likely to be greater when retrieval occurs closer to the time of the witnessed events. The conclusion above has important implications for law enforcement and the legal process and calls into question the validity of in-court identifications and their appropriateness as statements of fact.

Memory Retrieval

Memory retrieval refers to the process by which stored information is accessed and brought into consciousness, where it can be used to make decisions and guide actions. Retrieval of long-term declarative memories is often triggered through association with an external stimulus (i.e., a retrieval cue).[79] For example, the slight stubble on a lineup participant's face may be enough to elicit retrieval of a suspect's entire face. These same retrieval processes can also be engaged internally—a verbally triggered stream of thought related to a witnessed crime may readily bring to mind visual features of the perpetrator. A corollary of this association-based phenomenon is that memory retrieval is often context dependent; a memory may be more

---

[76]U. Rimmele et al., "Emotion Enhances the Subjective Feeling of Remembering, Despite Lower Accuracy for Contextual Details," *Emotion* 11(3): 553–562 (2011). Kensinger, "Remembering the Detail." Neisser and Harsh, *Affect and Accuracy in Recall*. E. A. Phelps and T. Sharot, "How (and Why) Emotion Enhances the Subjective Sense of Recollection," *Current Directions in Psychological Science* 17(2): 147–152 (2008).

[77]K. A. Houston et al., "The Emotional Eyewitness: The Effects of Emotion on Specific Aspects of Eyewitness Recall and Recognition Performance," *Emotion* 13(1): 118–128 (2013). R. B. Edelstein et al., "Emotion and Eyewitness Memory," in *Memory and Emotion*, ed. D. Reisberg and P. Hertel (New York: Oxford University Press, 2004): 308–346. S-A. Christianson, "Emotional Stress and Eyewitness Memory: A Critical Review," *Psychological Bulletin* 112(2): 284–309 (1992).

[78]M. S. Zaragoza and S. M. Lane, "Sources of Misattribution and Suggestibility of Eyewitness Memory," *Journal of Experimental Psychology: Learning, Memory, and Cognition* 20 (4): 934–945 (1994). W. C. Thompson, K. A. Clarke-Stewart, and S. J. Lepore, "What Did the Janitor Do? Suggestive Interviewing and the Accuracy of Children's Accounts," *Law and Human Behaviour* 21(4): 405–426 (1997). D. S. Lindsay and M. K. Johnson, "The Eyewitness Suggestibility Effect and Memory for Source," *Memory and Cognition* 17(3): 349–358 (1989).

[79]E. Tulving and Z. Pearlstone, "Availability Versus Accessibility of Information in Memory for Words," *Journal of Verbal Learning and Verbal Behaviour* 5: 381–391 (1966).

readily retrieved if the observer is in physical surroundings that are the same as or similar to those in which the original experiences took place (because the surroundings provide additional cues to trigger memory retrieval).[80]

Memory retrieval is heavily affected by various sources of noise. Similarities of meaning or appearance between retrieval cues and items in memory can easily lead to retrieval of the wrong item, producing a false memory.[81] This is particularly a problem given the categorical nature of memory.[82] The rugged mustachioed man in the lineup may lead to retrieval of the familiar categorical prototype—the Marlboro Man—rather than the specific person perceived at the scene of the crime, which in turn could interfere with or lead to errors in recognition (i.e., identification). Another type of memory retrieval failure is caused by "intrusion errors," in which information known to be commonly associated with events of a general type becomes incorporated into the retrieved content of a specific memory (and subsequently incorporated into the reconsolidated memory). For example, because guns are often associated with robbery, an observer may readily and unwittingly incorporate a gun into the retrieved version of his or her memory of a witnessed robbery.

Intrusion errors are one manifestation of a larger retrieval problem in which there is loss of information about the source of a memory. In cases of "source memory failure," we effectively forget how we know things (forget when and where we learned the content of our memories). What this means practically is that we may attribute later acquisition of information to earlier experiences. An eyewitness might learn from the police or some other source that a potential suspect has a moustache and then attribute

---

[80]D. Godden and A. Baddeley, "Context Dependent Memory in Two Natural Environments," *British Journal of Psychology* 66(3): 325–331 (1975). S. M. Smith and E. Vela, "Environmental Context-Dependent Eyewitness Recognition," *Applied Cognitive Psychology* 6: 125–139 (1992). S. M. Smith and E. Vela, "Environmental Context-Dependent Memory: A Review and Meta-Analysis," *Psychonomic Bulletin Review* 8 (2): 203–220 (2001). Tulving and Thomson, "Encoding Specificity and Retrieval Processes."

[81]J. R. Anderson, "A Spreading Activation Theory of Memory," *Journal of Verbal Learning and Verbal Behavior* 22(3): 261–295 (1983). A. M. Collins and E. F. Loftus, "A Spreading-Activation Theory of Semantic Processing," *Psychological Review* 82(6):407–428 (1975). H. L. Roediger III, D. A. Balota, and J. M. Watson, "Spreading Activation and Arousal of False Memories," in *The Nature of Remembering: Essays in Honor of Robert G. Crowder*, ed. H. L. Roediger III, J. Nairne, I. Neath, and A. Surprenant (Washington, DC: American Psychological Association, 2001): 95–115. C. J. Brainerd and V. F. Reyna, *The Science of False Memory* (New York: Oxford University Press, 2005).

[82]Tulving, "Episodic and Semantic Memory." M. J. Farah and J. L. McClelland, "A Computational Model of Semantic Memory Impairment: Modality Specificity and Emergent Category Specificity," *Journal of Experimental Psychology: General* 120(4): 339–357 (1991). G. W. Humphreys and E. M. Forde, "Hierarchies, Similarity, and Interactivity in Object Recognition: 'Category-Specific' Neuropsychological Deficits," *Behavioral and Brain Sciences* 24(3): 453–476 (2001).

that knowledge to the witnessed events, which may, in turn, have disastrous consequences for the ability of the eyewitness to accurately report what she or he has seen.

As for the processes of memory encoding and storage, the emotional content of memory also affects memory retrieval. As noted above, memory retrieval is commonly context dependent. A related and well-documented phenomenon that bears on emotional memories is *state dependent memory*, in which retrieval accuracy is best if the individual's cognitive state at the time of retrieval matches cognitive state at the time of encoding.[83] When memories have an emotional component, retrieval may be best when the individual is induced to a corresponding emotional state (*mood dependent memory*),[84] which is accomplished by verbally or physically placing him or her in the same context, and may offer a valuable investigative tool for probing eyewitness accounts.[85]

Recognition Memory

Recognition memory is a specific type of declarative memory retrieval in which a sensory stimulus (a "cue" stimulus) elicits a memory of the stimulus stored following a prior encounter and often the sequence of events involving the stimulus, the spatial context in which the stimulus was experienced, and the presence of other objects, people, or thoughts that had appeared with the stimulus during the event.[86] Recognition memory decisions are based on the retrieved memory evidence, which can be triggered by the stimulus and can also emerge from an active search of items

---

[83]D. W. Goodwin et al., "Alcohol and Recall: State-Dependent Effects in Man," *Science* 163(3873): 1358–1360 (1969). Tulving and Thomson, "Encoding Specificity and Retrieval Processes." *Psychological Review* 80(5): 352–373 (1973). E. Girden and E. Culler, "Conditioned Responses in Curarized Striate Muscle in Dogs," *Journal of Comparative Psychology* 23(2): 261–274 (1937). D. A. Overton, "State-Dependent or 'Dissociated' Learning Produced with Pentobarbital," *Journal of Comparative and Physiological Psychology* 57(1): 3–12 (1964).

[84]P. M. Kenealy, "Mood State-Dependent Retrieval: The Effects of Induced Mood on Memory Reconsidered," *The Quarterly Journal of Experimental Psychology Section A: Human Experimental Psychology* 50(2): 290–317 (1997). P. A. Lewis and H. D. Critchley, "Mood-Dependent Memory," *Trends in Cognitive Sciences* 7(10): 431–433 (2003). G. H. Bower, "Mood and Memory," *American Psychologist* 36(2): 129–148 (1981). F. I. M. Craik and R. S. Lockhart, "Levels of Processing: A Framework for Memory Research," *Journal of Verbal Learning and Verbal Behavior* 11(6):671–684 (1972). Kensinger, "Remembering the Detail." K. A. Leight and H. C. Ellis "Emotional Mood States, Strategies, and State-Dependency in Memory," *Journal of Verbal Learning and Verbal Behavior* 20(3): 251–266 (1981).

[85]S. M. Smith and E. Vela, "Environmental Context-Dependent Eyewitness Recognition," *Applied Cognitive Psychology* 6: 125–139 (1992).

[86]G. Mandler, "Recognizing: The Judgment of Previous Occurrence," *Psychological Review* 87(3): 252–271 (1980).

in memory. One factor affecting the strength of the evidence retrieved is the similarity between the cue stimulus and the stimulus or stimuli that was/were previously encountered during the event. An observer engaged in this process holds an implicit criterion for the strength of evidence required to reach a positive decision. In the case of eyewitness identification, this process is routinely elicited by viewing faces in a lineup. When the evidence retrieved is insufficient to reach a decision, this can lead to a cycle of ever-greater scrutiny of the cue stimulus and efforts to recollect additional details of the original event. Ultimately a decision must be made about whether the retrieved evidence is sufficient to declare that the stimulus was previously experienced (or previously experienced in the particular event of interest) or whether the stimulus is novel (or not from the event of interest). If a recognition event occurs—that is, if the memory search triggered by one of the faces in the lineup leads to a strong enough subjective experience that the face is familiar and/or the recollection of sufficient event details—then the witness may declare that they recognize the face as having been previously encountered. Recognition memory decisions can thus be thought of as the final stage in the process of eyewitness identification.

Because it is a form of memory retrieval, recognition memory is susceptible to all of the factors summarized above that are known to interfere with retrieval. Recognition memory differs from other forms of retrieval (such as recalling a phone number or a cake recipe), however, in that a comparison must be made between the retrieved evidence and a decision threshold. That is, as noted above, recognition judgments require a decision criterion, an understanding of which presents a unique set of challenges for eyewitness identification (and recognition memory, generally). In particular, an observer's report of recognition (or, in a lineup setting, of identification) is influenced not simply by the strength or quality of the recalled memory evidence. The report of recognition (identification of a lineup member) is also influenced by the level of evidence that the observer finds acceptable to reach such a decision, i.e., by his or her decision criterion, or bias. An observer who holds a liberal criterion will likely recognize many true targets (i.e., the guilty), but will frequently err by reporting recognition of many false targets (i.e., innocents). Conversely, an observer who holds a conservative criterion will avoid the problem of erroneous recognition (identification), but will fail to identify some true targets. Estimating (or controlling) the observer's decision criterion is thus a critical step in efforts to judge the validity of an identification (see also Chapter 5).

Recognition memory for faces differs greatly between familiar and unfamiliar faces.[87] Because we often identify familiar individuals with ease,

---

[87]P. J. B. Hancock, V. Bruce, and A. M. Burton, "Recognition of Unfamiliar Faces," *Trends in Cognitive Sciences* 4(9): 330–337 (2000).

we tend to think we are generally very good at face recognition. However, we are not as good with unfamiliar faces.[88] All of the sources of noise that influence perception and memory contribute to these difficulties, and they are exacerbated by the attempts by criminals to conceal their identity (even a change in hairstyle and clothing can have a major effect on recognition).

The ability to recognize unfamiliar faces differs widely across individuals. At one extreme are those people, referred to as "super recognizers," who rarely forget a face.[89] At the other end of the spectrum are "face-blind people (prosopagnosics)," who have great difficulty recognizing even highly familiar faces.[90] Current estimates of the fraction of the general population afflicted by prosopagnosia are as high as ~2 percent.[91] The ability of an eyewitness to identify a suspect may thus differ greatly from individual to individual simply as a consequence of general variations in face recognition ability.

CONCLUSION

The shortcomings of eyewitness identification present a societal problem that has profound implications for our systems of law and justice. Ultimately, a solution to this problem must be informed by a thorough understanding of human vision and memory. The processes of vision and memory, which are fundamental to human experience, have been frequent targets of scientific investigation since the 19th century. The past few decades have seen an explosion of additional research that has led to important insights into how vision and memory work, what we see and remember best, and what causes these processes to fail. The committee has reviewed much of this research, as it pertains to eyewitness identification, and has identified restrictions on what can be seen under specific environmental and behavioral conditions (e.g., as poor illumination, limited viewing duration, viewing angle), factors that impede the ability to attend to critically informative features of a visual scene (e.g., the deleterious effect of an attention-grabbing element, such as a weapon, on the ability to correctly perceive the features of the assailant's face), distortions of perceptual experience derived from expectations, and ways in which emotion and stress enhance or suppress specific perceptual experiences. Memory is often far

---

[88]V. Bruce, "Changing Faces: Visual and Non-Visual Coding Processes in Face Recognition," *British Journal of Psychology* 73: 105–116 (1982).

[89]R. Russell, B. Duchaine, and K. Nakayama, "Super-Recognisers: People with Extraordinary Face Recognition Ability," *Psychonomic Bulletin and Review* 16(2): 252–272 (2009).

[90]T. Susilo and B. Ducahine, "Advances in Developmental Prosopagnosia Research," *Current Opinion in Neurobiology* 2(3):423–429 (2013).

[91]I. Kennerknecht et al., "First Report of Prevalence of Nonsyndromic Hereditary Prosopagnosia (HPA)," *American Journal of Medical Genetics Part A* 140(15): 1617–1622 (2006).

from a faithful record of what was perceived through the sense of sight: its contents can be forgotten or contaminated at multiple stages, it can be biased by the very practices designed to elicit recall, and it is heavily swayed by emotional states associated with witnessed events and their recall. From this analysis, the committee must conclude that there are insurmountable limits on vision and memory imposed by our biological nature and the properties of the world we inhabit. With this knowledge, it is possible to more fully appreciate the value and risks associated with eyewitness reports and accordingly advise those who collect, handle, defend, consider, and adjudicate such reports.

5

Applied Eyewitness Identification Research

The committee was tasked with (1) critically assessing the existing body of scientific research on eyewitness identification; (2) identifying gaps in the literature; and (3) suggesting other research that would further the understanding of eyewitness identification and improve law enforcement and courtroom practice. Eyewitness identification research resides in both the scientific literature and the law and justice-related scholarly literature. Although experiential, anecdotal, and some administrative records from law enforcement and the judiciary could contribute to a better understanding of eyewitness identification, the committee did not comprehensively review this more qualitative material. The committee did, however, examine select examples of law enforcement policies and influential judicial rulings.

In late 2013, the committee compiled an extensive and comprehensive bibliography from the following nine electronic databases, with the search limited to publications over the past two decades (i.e., since 1993): Academic Search Premier (EBSCO), Embase (Elsevier), MEDLINE (National Library of Medicine), NCJRS Abstracts Database (U.S. Department of Justice), PsycINFO (American Psychological Association), PubMed (National Institutes of Health), Scopus (Elsevier), Web of Science (Thomson Reuters), and LexisNexis.[1] Papers were drawn from such fields as social science, cognitive science, behavioral science, neuroscience, criminology, and law

---

[1] The law review literature was represented by the citations from the LexisNexis search. While all these materials were not reviewed in detail, several of the documents informed Chapter 3 of this report (The Legal Framework for Assessment of Eyewitness Identification).

using Boolean-logic-based search strategies designed to identify empirical research reports, review articles, systematic reviews, meta-analyses, and articles in law reviews and legal journals.

The committee concentrated its review on the subset of the bibliography deemed most important to its task, focusing more on the scientific literature than on the law review literature. These materials included meta-analyses and systematic reviews and primary research in neuroscience, statistics, and eyewitness identification. This report also was informed by several early foundational papers and written comments from, and presentations to, the committee by representatives from science, law enforcement, state courts and government, private organizations, and other interested parties. The comments and presentations revealed additional highly relevant new findings, some recently published or in press and others in submission. The agenda for each committee meeting is available in Appendix B. All materials submitted to the committee are retained in the Academies' public access file and are available upon request.

COMMITTEE ASSESSMENT

Many factors affect eyewitness accuracy. Some factors are related to protocols within the law enforcement and legal systems, while others are related to characteristics associated with the crime scene, perpetrator, and witness.

System variables are those that the criminal justice system can influence through the enforcement of standards and through education and training of law enforcement personnel in the use of best practices[2] and procedures (e.g., by specifying the content and nature of instructions given to witnesses prior to a lineup identification). Estimator variables include factors operating either at the time of the criminal event (relating to visual experience or memory encoding) or during the retention interval (the time between witnessing an event and the identification process). Specific examples include the eyewitness' level of stress or trauma at the time of the incident, the light level and nature of the visual conditions that affect visibility and clarity of a perpetrator's features, similarity of age and race of the witness and perpetrator, presence or absence of a weapon during the incident, and the physical distance separating the witness from the perpetrator.

A scientific consensus about the effects of some factors has emerged, but no such consensus exists for many other factors. One method of assessing scientific consensus is by surveys of experts. A 2001 survey collected

---

[2]As noted in Chapter 1, for the purposes of this report, the committee characterizes *best practice* as the adoption of standardized procedures based on scientific principles. The committee does not make any endorsement of practices designated as best practices by other bodies.

responses from 64 psychologists about their courtroom experiences and their opinions on 30 eyewitness-related phenomena to determine the "general acceptance" of these phenomena within the eyewitness identification research community.[3] General acceptance is relevant to whether scientific testimony is admissible as evidence in court (see Chapter 3). The survey revealed substantial agreement about which findings these experts felt were sufficiently reliable to present in court.[4]

The committee examined the scientific literature on eyewitness identification, focusing first on quantitative syntheses, largely systematic reviews and meta-analyses, which were identified in a comprehensive search of electronic databases designed to locate research on both estimator and system variables. In addition, primary research studies were identified in this database search, many of which were also highlighted in the relevant systematic reviews and meta-analyses. Finally, some researchers forwarded manuscripts to the committee that have been submitted for peer-review or are in press. In their examination of this body of literature, the committee examined the quality of the identified research and, where possible, worked to derive summary empirical generalizations related to variables of interest.

Quantitative Syntheses of Eyewitness Identification Research

The committee first evaluated the consistency of research findings across studies for system and estimator variables by studying published quantitative reviews of empirical research. Systematic reviews, which collect and appraise available research on specific hypotheses or research questions, are efforts to synthesize the effects of variables across studies. Within systematic reviews, meta-analysis is often, but not always, used to compute the effects of variables as well as to identify factors that explain differences across studies. When assumptions about consistency of data collected across studies are met, meta-analysis provides a quantitative summary of empirical findings by statistically averaging effect sizes across individual studies, thereby increasing the precision of the effect size estimate as well

---

[3]S. M. Kassin et al., "On the 'General Acceptance' of Eyewitness Testimony Research: A New Survey of the Experts," *American Psychologist* 56(5): 405–416 (2001).

[4]Kassin et al. also compared the reliability assessments of the 2001 survey to assessments from a similar 1989 survey and noted that, for the 17 propositions retested, there was a remarkable degree of consistency: "most experts saw as sufficiently reliable expert testimony on the wording of questions," lineup instructions, attitudes and expectations, the accuracy-confidence correlation, the forgetting curve, exposure time, and unconscious transference. "There was less, if any, consensus on the effects of color perception in monochromatic light," "observer training, high levels of stress, the accuracy of hypnotically refreshed testimony, and event violence." The authors observed that two phenomena were seen as significantly more reliable than had been the case when the initial survey was conducted: weapon focus effect and hypnotic suggestibility effects. See p. 410.

as the statistical power to detect effects. Done well, systematic reviews with or without meta-analysis provide evidence for practice and policy for such fields as health care,[5] crime and justice, social welfare, and education.[6] The utility of systematic reviews for informing practice and policy is predicated on the included studies being transparently reported, conducted so as to minimize risk of bias, and representing as complete a sample as possible of research conducted on the central question, including both published and unpublished studies. In turn, systematic reviews should specify inclusion criteria and data extraction procedures a priori, use independent and duplicate procedures for study selection and data extraction, rigorously evaluate potential biases in included studies, and interpret results of meta-analyses in terms that are useful to decision-makers. Further, meta-analyses should not be conducted outside the context of systematic reviews. In short, both systematic reviews and the studies they include need to be transparent and reproducible in order to best inform practice and policy decisions about eyewitness identification.

The committee examined quantitative reviews that covered decades of research on both estimator variables (exposure duration,[7] retention interval,[8] stress,[9] weapon focus,[10] own-race bias,[11] and own-age bias[12]) and system variables (identification test medium, i.e., live lineup versus photo array,[13]

[5] See the Cochrane Collaboration, available at: http://www.cochrane.org.

[6] See the Campbell Collaboration, available at: http://www.campbellcollaboration.org.

[7] B. H. Bornstein et al., "Effects of Exposure Time and Cognitive Operations on Facial Identification Accuracy: A Meta-Analysis of Two Variables Associated with Initial Memory Strength," *Psychology, Crime and Law* 18(5): 473–490 (2012).

[8] K. A. Deffenbacher et al., "Forgetting the Once-Seen Face: Estimating the Strength of an Eyewitness's Memory Representation," *Journal of Experimental Psychology: Applied* 14(2): 139–150 (2008).

[9] K. A. Deffenbacher et al., "A Meta-Analytic Review of the Effects of High Stress on Eyewitness Memory," *Law and Human Behavior* 28(6): 687–706 (2004).

[10] J. M. Fawcett et al., "Of Guns and Geese: A Meta-Analytic Review of the 'Weapon Focus' Literature," *Psychology, Crime and Law* 19(1): 35–66 (2013).

[11] C. A. Meissner and J. C. Brigham, "Thirty Years of Investigating the Own-Race Bias in Memory for Faces—A Meta-Analytic Review," *Psychology, Public Policy, and Law* 7(1): 3–35 (2001).

[12] M. G. Rhodes and J. S. Anastasi, "The Own-Age Bias in Face Recognition: A Meta-Analytic and Theoretical Review," *Psychological Bulletin* 138(1): 146–174 (2012).

[13] B. L. Cutler et al., "Conceptual, Practical, and Empirical Issues Associated with Eyewitness Identification Test Media," in *Adult Eyewitness Testimony: Current Trends and Developments*, ed. D. F. Ross (New York: Press Syndicate of the University of Cambridge, 1994), 163–181.

biased and unbiased lineup instructions,[14] post-identification feedback,[15] simultaneous versus sequential lineup presentation,[16] target absent versus target present lineups,[17] foil similarity,[18] blinding,[19] showup versus lineup,[20] prior mug shot exposure,[21] verbal description and identification,[22] and the cognitive interview[23]). Many of these quantitative reviews were published recently, with more than one-third published since 2010. However, none of the reviews met all current standards for conducting and reporting sys-

---

[14]S. E. Clark, "A Re-Examination of the Effects of Biased Lineup Instructions in Eyewitness Identification," *Law and Human Behavior* 29(4): 395–424 (2005). S. E. Clark, "Costs and Benefits of Eyewitness Identification Reform: Psychological Science and Public Policy," *Perspectives on Psychological Science* 7(3): 238–259 (2012). N. K. Steblay, "Social Influence in Eyewitness Recall: A Meta-Analytic Review of Lineup Instruction Effects," *Law and Human Behavior* 21(3): 283–297 (1997). N. K. Steblay, G. L. Wells, and A. B. Douglass, "The Eyewitness Post Identification Feedback Effect 15 Years Later: Theoretical and Policy Implications," *Psychology, Public Policy, and Law* 20(1): 1–18 (2014).

[15]S. E. Clark and R. D. Godfrey, "Eyewitness Identification Evidence and Innocence Risk," *Psychonomic Bulletin and Review* 16(1): 22–42 (2009). A. B. Douglass and N. K. Steblay, "Memory Distortion in Eyewitnesses: A Meta-Analysis of the Post-Identification Feedback Effect," *Applied Cognitive Psychology* 20(7): 859–869 (2006).

[16]Clark, "Costs and Benefits of Eyewitness Identification Reform." S. E. Clark, R. T. Howell, and S. L. Davey, "Regularities in Eyewitness Identification," *Law and Human Behavior* 32(3): 187–218 (2008). N. K. Steblay et al., "Eyewitness Accuracy Rates In Sequential and Simultaneous Lineup Presentations: A Meta-Analytic Comparison," *Law and Human Behavior* 25(5): 459–473 (2001). N. K. Steblay et al., "Seventy-two Tests of the Sequential Lineup Superiority Effect: A Meta-Analysis and Policy Discussion," *Psychology, Public Policy, and Law* 17(1): 99–139 (2011).

[17]Clark, "A Re-Examination of the Effects of Biased Lineup Instructions in Eyewitness Identification." Clark, Howell, and Davey, "Regularities in Eyewitness Identification." Clark and Godfrey, "Eyewitness Identification Evidence and Innocence Risk."

[18]Clark, "Costs and Benefits of Eyewitness Identification Reform." Clark and Godfrey, "Eyewitness Identification Evidence and Innocence Risk." Clark, Howell, and Davey, "Regularities in Eyewitness Identification." R. J. Fitzgerald et al., "The Effect of Suspect-Filler Similarity on Eyewitness Identification Decisions: A Meta-Analysis," *Psychology, Public Policy, and Law* 19(2): 151–164 (2013). S. L. Sporer et al., "Choosing, Confidence, and Accuracy: A Meta-Analysis of the Confidence-Accuracy Relation in Eyewitness Identification Studies," *Psychological Bulletin* 118(3): 315–327 (1995).

[19]Clark, "Costs and Benefits of Eyewitness Identification Reform."

[20]Clark, "Costs and Benefits of Eyewitness Identification Reform." N. K. Steblay et al., "Eyewitness Accuracy Rates in Police Showup and Lineup Presentations: A Meta-Analytic Comparison," *Law and Human Behavior* 27(5): 523–540 (2003).

[21]K. A. Deffenbacher et al., "Mugshot Exposure Effects: Retroactive Interference, Mugshot Commitment, Source Confusion, and Unconscious Transference," *Law and Human Behavior* 30(3): 287–307 (2006).

[22]C. A. Meissner, S. L Sporer, and K. J. Susa, "A Theoretical Review and Meta-Analysis of the Description-Identification Relationship in Memory for Faces," *European Journal of Cognitive Psychology* 20(3): 414–455 (2008).

[23]A. Memon et al., "The Cognitive Interview: A Meta-Analytic Review and Study Space Analysis of the Past 25 Years," *Psychology, Public Policy, and Law* 16(4): 340–372 (2010).

tematic reviews,[24] and few met even a majority of these standards, making assessment of the credibility of their findings problematic.

After examining the reviews, the committee concluded that the findings may be subject to unintended biases and that the conclusions are less credible than was hoped. In many cases, the data from the studies cited were not readily available or were not clearly presented. Nevertheless, these reviews were helpful in highlighting some of the issues associated with specific research questions and in identifying primary studies that might be both credible and important.

RESEARCH STUDIES ON SYSTEM VARIABLES

After its assessment of the systematic reviews and meta-analytic studies, the committee's review focused on the most-studied system variables. Key system variables, such as lineup procedures (e.g., simultaneous vs. sequential lineups, blinded vs. non-blinded lineup administration) and the collection/use of witness confidence statements, can have a marked influence over the validity of eyewitness identifications. In the following section, one of the most important practical issues raised by this influence is addressed: What is the best way to evaluate the effects of system variables on the diagnostic accuracy of eyewitness reports, and how might we use the results of such an evaluation to optimize the states of key system variables and thus maximize performance of an eyewitness? This question is, in principle, relevant to all system variables, but we address it first in the timely and controversial context of simultaneous versus sequential lineup presentations and in the role of eyewitness confidence judgments in evaluation of identification performance. This examination of lineup procedures and confidence reports is followed by a brief discussion of the effects on eyewitness performance of another important system variable: the extent and content of communications between the witness and the larger community (law enforcement, legal defense, the press, family and friends, etc.).

Evaluating Eyewitness Performance

Perhaps the most important empirical question that can be asked about eyewitness identification is: How well do witnesses perform as a function of different system and estimator variables? For example, do factors such as the structure of a lineup, stress, or weapon focus affect the ability of

---

[24]See, e.g., Institute of Medicine, *Finding What Works in Health Care: Standards for Systematic Reviews* (Washington, DC: The National Academies Press, 2011) and B. J. Shea et al., *Development of AMSTAR: A Measurement Tool to Assess the Methodological Quality of Systematic Reviews*, BMC Medical Research Methodology 2007, 7:10 doi:10.1186/1471-2288-7-10.

a witness to provide reliable information? If so, what practices will yield the best performance? The issues are multifaceted, and the answers likely depend upon many factors. Given the complexity of these issues, the experimental literature to date has focused largely on one of the more tractable problems: How do different lineup identification procedures affect witness identifications? The committee will use this focus (and its eminent practical relevance) to illustrate how one might go about evaluating eyewitness performance generally.

Most lineup identification procedures take one of two forms: *simultaneous* or *sequential*. In a simultaneous procedure, the witness views all individuals in the lineup at the same time and either identifies one (or more) as the perpetrator or reports that the person she or he saw at the crime scene was not in the lineup. In a sequential procedure, the witness views individuals one at a time and reports whether or not each one is the person from the crime scene. Rigorous evaluation of eyewitness identification performance as a function of these two procedures requires a formal understanding of the task that the witness confronts, and it requires criteria for assessing the outcome.

The task of a witness viewing a lineup is an example of what is known as a binary classification problem.[25] Each eyewitness faces two possible (binary) states associated with each person in the lineup (guilt or innocence), and the witness must assign each person to one of two classes (guilty or innocent). For each decision, the witness can be correct or incorrect, yielding four possible outcomes: a correct classification as guilty ("hit"), an incorrect classification as guilty ("false alarm"), a correct classification as innocent ("correct rejection"), and an incorrect classification as innocent ("miss"). These outcomes are commonly presented in a contingency table[26] (see Figure 5-1), and the frequencies in each part of that table are the raw data used to evaluate performance on a binary classification task, such as eyewitness identification.[27]

There are many different performance measures that can be derived from data of this sort—indeed, the fields of statistical classification and machine learning are replete with tools for the evaluation of binary classifiers.[28]

---

[25]The binary classifier in this context is defined as the witness operating under a specific set of conditions, such as lineup procedures.

[26]Also termed "confusion matrix."

[27]The prevalence or "base-rate"—the fraction of individuals in each category (guilty or innocent, in the eyewitness problem) in the population is also a factor that may come into play when evaluating binary classification performance.

[28]See, e.g., T. Hastie, R. Tibshirani, and J. H. Friedman, *The Elements of Statistical Learning: Data Mining, Inference, and Prediction* (New York: Springer, 2009) and A. Smola and S. V. N. Vishwanathan, *Introduction to Machine Learning* (Cambridge: Cambridge University Press, 2008).

Witness Classification of Lineup Participant

		guilty	innocent
True Status of Lineup Participant	guilty	"Hit" (true positive)	"Miss" (false negative)
	innocent	"False Alarm" (false positive)	"Correct Rejection" (true negative)

FIGURE 5-1 Contingency table for possible eyewitness identification outcomes. SOURCE: Courtesy of Thomas D. Albright.

The preferred measure will depend to a large degree upon the criteria one adopts for performance evaluation.

Perhaps the simplest measure of binary classification performance is the ratio of hit rates (HR) to false alarm rates (FAR), i.e., HR/FAR.[29] The magnitude of this measure, which is known in the eyewitness identification literature as the "diagnosticity ratio," is proportional to the likelihood that a classification is correct, i.e., that the person identified as guilty is actually guilty.[30] The diagnosticity ratio is appealing if the most critical criterion is avoiding erroneous identifications.

---

[29]The "rate" associated with each cell of the contingency table is computed as the number of counts within that cell (e.g., number of people correctly classified as guilty) divided by the number of instances that are truly in that class (e.g., total number of guilty people being classified). Thus, hit rates (HR) = number of hits / (number of hits+number of misses), and false alarm rate (FAR) = number of false alarms / (number of false alarms+number of correct rejections).

[30]The "diagnosticity ratio" is also known in other disciplines by other names; e.g., "positive likelihood ratio" or "LR+ = Likelihood Ratio of a Positive Call;" see Peter Lee, *Bayesian Statistics: An Introduction* (Chichester: Wiley, 2012), Sec 4.1.

Not surprisingly, the diagnosticity ratio was adopted in pioneering efforts to identify lineup conditions that would yield better witness identification performance.[31] Most laboratory-based studies and meta-analyses of the effects of lineup procedures on eyewitness identification performance show that, with standard lineup instructions informing the witness that the perpetrator may or may not be present, the sequential procedure produces a higher diagnosticity ratio.[32] That is, when considering only those cases in which a witness actually selects someone from a lineup, the ratio of correct to false identifications is commonly higher with the sequential than with the simultaneous procedure.[33]

A higher diagnosticity ratio could result from a higher hit rate, a lower false alarm rate, or some combination of the two. Some early reports suggested that sequential procedures (relative to simultaneous) lead to fewer false alarms without changing the frequency of hits, which would result in a higher diagnosticity ratio.[34] More recent laboratory-based studies and meta-analyses typically show that sequential procedures (relative to simultaneous) are associated with a somewhat reduced hit rate accompanied by a larger reduction in the false alarm rate, thereby resulting in diagnosticity ratios higher than those yielded by simultaneous procedures.[35] In other

[31]R. C. L. Lindsay and G. L. Wells, "Improving Eyewitness Identifications from Lineups: Simultaneous Versus Sequential Lineup Presentation," *Journal of Applied Psychology* 70(3), 556–564 (1985).

[32]Steblay et al. "Eyewitness Accuracy Rates in Sequential and Simultaneous Lineup Presentations." Steblay, et al., "Seventy-two Tests of the Sequential Lineup Superiority Effect." S. D. Gronlund et al., "Robustness of the Sequential Lineup Advantage," *Journal of Experimental Psychology: Applied* 15(2): 140–152 (2009). S. D. Gronlund, J. T. Wixted, and L. Mickes, "Evaluating Eyewitness Identification Procedures Using ROC Analysis," *Current Directions in Psychological Science* 23(1): 3–10 (2014).

[33]But see C. A. Carlson, S. D. Gronlund, and S. E. Clark, "Lineup Composition, Suspect Position, and the Sequential Lineup Advantage," *Journal of Experimental Psychology-Applied* 14(2): 118-128 (2008), for a counterexample. Also, Clark, Moreland, and Gronlund have demonstrated that the accuracy advantage of sequential lineups as measured by diagnosticity ratios has decreased over time since the original report. Reanalysis of diagnosticity data for sequential studies showed slight, non-significant decreases in correct identification effects and increases in false identification effects, which together combine to produce a significant decrease in the advantage of sequential over simultaneous lineup methods. See S. E. Clark, M. B. Moreland, and S. D. Gronlund, "Evolution of the Empirical and Theoretical Foundations of Eyewitness Identification Reform," *Psychonomic Bulletin and Review* 21(2): 251–267 (2014).

[34]R. C. L. Lindsay, "Applying Applied Research: Selling the Sequential Lineup," *Applied Cognitive Psychology* 13(3): 219–225 (1999). G. L. Wells, S. M. Rydell, and E. P. Seelau, "The Selection of Distractors for Eyewitness Lineups," *Journal of Applied Psychology* 78(5): 835–844 (1993).

[35]A recent field-based study comparing sequential to simultaneous procedures in a limited number of jurisdictions computed the diagnosticity ratio using filler identifications as the false alarm rate (because the innocence or guilt of the suspect is unknown in such situations). See G. L. Wells, N. K. Steblay, J. E. Dysart, "Double-Blind Photo-Lineups Using Actual

words, when using a single diagnosticity ratio as a measure of eyewitness performance, the sequential procedure (relative to simultaneous) comes closer to satisfying the popular criterion that those identified as guilty are actually guilty. In light of these findings, many policy makers have advocated sequential procedures, and those procedures have been adopted by law enforcement in many jurisdictions.

While policy decisions and practice have been influenced by the aforementioned studies, there are other criteria worthy of consideration when evaluating eyewitness performance. One alternative is revealed by asking *why* the diagnosticity ratio changes across lineup conditions. This question can be addressed given a plausible model of the mechanisms underlying human recognition memory. Most models of recognition memory are based on the idea that a cue (e.g., a face in a lineup) results in the retrieval of information stored in memory (see Chapter 4). When the retrieved information provides enough evidence to satisfy the observer, they make an identification—that is, they decide that the stimulus is "recognized." Explicit in this model are two important parameters: the observer's memory sensitivity (that is, the "discriminability" between the strength of memory evidence elicited by a previously encountered stimulus and that elicited by novel stimuli), and the degree of evidence that the observer requires to make an identification ("response criterion" or "bias") (see Box 5-1).

The first of these two parameters—discriminability—is important for evaluating eyewitness performance. It tells whether a difference in performance under different task conditions reflects a true improvement in memory-based discrimination, i.e., *an improvement in the strength of the observer's retrieved memory evidence of the perpetrator*.

The fact that these two measures (the likelihood that an identified person is guilty vs. discriminability) do not assess the same thing is counterintuitive—a fact that has generated controversy in the field of eyewitness

---

Eyewitnesses: An Experimental Test of a Sequential versus Simultaneous Lineup Procedure," *Law and Human Behavior*, 15 June 2014, doi: 10.1037/lhb0000096. When computed in this manner, the data revealed a modest diagnosticity ratio advantage for the sequential procedure. However, Amendola and Wixted re-analyzed a subset of the data for which proxy measures of ground truth were available [K. Amendola and J. T. Wixted, "Comparing the Diagnostic Accuracy of Suspect Identifications Made by Actual Eyewitnesses from Simultaneous and Sequential Lineups," accepted by *Journal of Experimental Criminology* (2014)]. Their analyses suggested that identification of innocent suspects is less likely and identification of guilty suspects is more likely when using the simultaneous procedures. While future field studies are needed, these latter findings raise the possibility that diagnosticity is higher for the simultaneous procedure. See also Clark, Moreland, and Gronlund, who report that published diagnosticity ratios have changed over time, reflecting a significant decrease in the advantage of sequential over simultaneous lineup procedures. (Clark, Moreland, and Gronlund, "Evolution of the Empirical and Theoretical Foundations of Eyewitness Identification Reform.")

BOX 5-1
The Influences of Discriminability and Response Bias on Human Binary Classification Decisions

All human decisions about the classification of objects based on memory—including a witness' classifications of guilt or innocence for faces in a lineup, an individual's decision as to whether a piece of luggage is his or her own, a botanist's recognition of a specific type of fern, a radiologist's detection of a tumor in a mammogram, or the determination of the sex of a newly-hatched chicken—can be distilled down to the influence of two factors that are rooted in causal models of recognition memory:the degree to which the relevant objects are discriminable by the decider (the decider's *sensitivity* to the difference between them), and the decider's criterion for making a decision (response bias, or the decider's degree of *specificity* in making choices).[a] There are, of course, many other variables that will affect the outcome (e.g., levels of stress, attentional focus, potential rewards or expectations), but all of these are believed to exert their influence over memory-based classification decisions by affecting discriminability and/or response bias.

To illustrate the distinction between discrimination and response bias as applied to a real-world decision problem, consider how an audiologist conducts a hearing test. In a hearing test, an individual might be asked to detect sounds along a continuum of loudness and to indicate when a sound is present. The audiologist wants to know how well someone can discriminate presence versus absence of a sound, but that assessment is complicated by the criterion people use when deciding to say that they heard a sound (response bias). Some people are hesitant to respond positively, saying "I hear it" only when they are absolutely certain ("conservative" responders). Others are more willing to respond positively, saying "I hear it" with less information and greater uncertainty ("liberal" responders). Those with a conservative bias are less likely to report hearing a sound in general, so they will have both fewer correct detections ("hits") and fewer overt mistakes ("false alarms"). By contrast, those with a liberal bias are more likely to say that they heard a sound, so they will have more hits but also more false alarms. Importantly, this can occur even if the conservative and liberal responders do not differ in their ability to discriminate the presence or absence of sound.

---

[a]See, e.g., W. P. Banks, "Signal Detection Theory and Human Memory," *Psychological Bulletin* 74(2): 81–99 (1970); J. P. Egan, *Recognition Memory and the Operating Characteristic* (Bloomington: Indiana University Hearing and Communication Laboratory, 1958); D. M. Green and J. A. Swets, *Signal Detection Theory and Psychophysics* (New York: Wiley,1966).

identification research.[36] Intuitively, if sequential lineups yield a higher
likelihood that an identified person is guilty (as quantified by a higher
diagnosticity ratio), then it seems as if that procedure yields objectively
better performance. The problem with this intuition is that it fails to take
into account the second of the two parameters of recognition memory
models—the response bias or degree of evidence that the observer finds acceptable to make an identification. This parameter, which is distinct from
discriminability, reflects the witness' tendency to pick or not to pick someone from the lineup. If a witness sets a high bar for acceptable evidence—a
conservative bias—then he or she will be unlikely to select anyone from
the lineup (low pick frequency), meaning that they will have more misses
(will be more likely to fail to select the suspect because they are less likely
to make a selection at all) and fewer false alarms.

Conversely, if a witness sets a low bar for acceptable evidence—a liberal
bias—then she or he will be more likely to make a selection from the lineup
(a high pick frequency), meaning he or she will have more hits and will
make more false identifications. Differences in pick frequency can, and generally do, lead to differences in the ratio of hit rates to false alarm rates; all
else being equal, the diagnosticity ratio will be higher for a conservative bias
than for a liberal bias.[37] In other words, simply by inducing a witness to
adopt a more conservative bias, it is possible to increase the likelihood that
an identified person is actually guilty. Importantly, this may be true even
if the procedure yields no better, or potentially worse, discriminability.[38]

Despite its merits, a single diagnosticy ratio thus conflates the influences
of discriminability and response bias on binary classification, which mud-
dies the determination of which procedure, if any, yields objectively better
discriminability in eyewitness performance. To overcome this problem,
some investigators have recently adopted a technique from signal detection

---

[36] See, e.g., J. T. Wixted and L. Mickes, "The Field of Eyewitness Memory Should Aban-
don Probative Value and Embrace Receiver Operating Characteristic Analysis," *Perspectives
on Psychological Science* 7(3): 275-278 (2012); Clark, "Costs and Benefits of Eyewitness
Identification Reform"; G. L. Wells, "Eyewitness Identification Probative Value, Criterion
Shifts, and Policy Regarding the Sequential Lineup," *Current Directions in Psychological
Science* 23(1): 11–16 (2014); and Steblay, et al. "Seventy-two Tests of the Sequential Lineup
Superiority Effect."

[37] The sole exception to this rule is the case in which classifications are made at chance level
of performance, i.e., when the observer exhibits no ability to discriminate.

[38] L. Mickes, H. D. Flowe, and J. T. Wixted, "Receiver Operating Characteristic Analysis of
Eyewitness Memory: Comparing the Diagnostic Accuracy of Simultaneous vs. Sequential Lineups," *Journal of Experimental Psychology: Applied* 18 (4): 361–376 (2012). C. A. Meissner
et al., "Eyewitness Decisions In Simultaneous and Sequential Lineups: A Dual Process Signal
Detection Theory Analysis," *Memory and Cognition* 33(5): 783–792 (2005). M. A. Palmer
and N. Brewer, "Sequential Lineup Presentation Promotes Less-Biased Criterion Setting but
Does Not Improve Discriminability," *Law and Human Behavior* 36(3): 247–255 (2012).

theory, which distinguishes the relative influences of discriminability and bias on binary classification.[39] This technique involves analysis of Receiver Operating Characteristics (see Box 5-2). ROC analysis has been used extensively in multiple contexts of human decision-making, notably in basic research on visual perception and memory and applied studies of medical diagnostic procedures.[40] In essence, ROC analysis examines diagnosticity ratios integrated over different response biases. This approach to eyewitness research has been promoted based on the claim that it can enable lineup procedures to be evaluated by their effect on discrimination, separate from response bias, and—importantly—because the dimensions of analysis (discriminability and response bias) correspond to the mechanistic parameters of causal models of human recognition memory.

Use of ROC analysis to evaluate eyewitness performance requires calculating the diagnosticity ratio for different response bias conditions (see Box 5-2). Using expressed confidence level (ECL) as a proxy for response bias (see below), a small set of recent studies using ROC analysis has reported that discriminability (area under the ROC curve) for simultaneous lineups is as high, or higher, than that for sequential lineups.[41] In other words, when eyewitness identification performance is evaluated based on a criterion of bias-free discriminability, the results differ from those based on a single diagnosticity ratio, and they do so because the latter fails to account for response bias.

Looking broadly at the many empirical studies that have used a single diagnosticity ratio to evaluate eyewitness performance, as well as the more recent findings using ROC analysis, it appears that the practical advantage of one lineup procedure over another depends to a large degree upon the performance criterion that one adopts. From the perspective of many, the ideal lineup procedure would elicit a conservative bias (thus reducing false identifications) and high discriminability (that is, optimizing memory sensitivity). If there exists no discriminability advantage for one lineup

---

[39]D. M. Green and J. A. Swets, *Signal Detection Theory and Psychophysics* (New York: Wiley, 1966); D. McNicol, *A Primer of Signal Detection Theory* (London: George Allen and Unwin, 1972).

[40]J. A. Swets, "ROC Analysis Applied to the Evaluation of Medical Imaging Techniques," *Investigative Radiology* 14(2): 109–121 (1979).

[41] Mickes, Flowe, and Wixted, "Receiver Operating Characteristic Analysis of Eyewitness Memory." C. A. Carlson and M. A. Carlson, "An Evaluation of Lineup Presentation, Weapon Presence, and a Distinctive Feature Using ROC Analysis," *Journal of Applied Research in Memory and Cognition* 3(2): 45–53 (2014). D. G. Dobolyi and C. S. Dodson, "Eyewitness Confidence in Simultaneous and Sequential Lineups: A Criterion Shift Account for Sequential Mistaken Identification Overconfidence," *Journal of Experimental Psychology: Applied* 19 (4): 345–357 (2013). S. D. Gronlund et al., "Showups Versus Lineups: An Evaluation Using ROC Analysis," *Journal of Applied Research in Memory and Cognition* 1(4): 221–228 (2012).

BOX 5-2
Analysis of Receiver Operating Characteristics (ROCs)

Binary classification decisions by human observers are affected by both discriminability (the observer's sensitivity to the difference between target and non-targets) and response bias (the observer's degree of specificity in making a response). Analysis of Receiver Operating Characteristics (ROCs) is a method from signal detection theory that enables one to distinguish the relative influences of discriminability and response bias on binary classification decisions. ROC analysis is performed by plotting the frequency of decisions that are hits (correctly detecting a target) versus the frequency of decisions that are false alarms (incorrectly classifying a non-target as a target).

The positive diagonal in an ROC plot (see figure next page) corresponds to response bias, moving from high specificity at the lower left corner [no detection of targets (hit rate = 0) and no incorrect attribution of non-targets as targets (false alarm rate = 0)], to low specificity at the upper right corner [all targets detected (hit rate = 1.0) and all non-targets attributed as targets (false alarm rate = 1.0)]. Because all points along this positive diagonal reflect equal ratios of hits to false alarms, they vary in response bias (i.e., the frequency of lineup picks, or "pick frequency"), but they do not manifest differences in discriminability. The negative diagonal in an ROC plot corresponds, by contrast, to discriminability, moving from chance discriminability at the intersection with the positive diagonal, where hits and false alarms are equally likely, to the highest discriminability in the upper left corner, where all targets are detected (hit rate = 1.0), but no non-targets are attributed as targets (false alarm rate = 0).

To see how measured hit and false alarm rates vary over different conditions of discriminability and response bias in laboratory experiments, one can manipulate or estimate these conditions and record a diagnosticity ratio (HR/FAR) for each condition. The typical result is a set of diagnosticity ratios that, when plotted in the ROC space (represented by the dots in the figure at right), form a curve spanning from lower left to upper right. The extent to which that curve deviates (bows above and away) from the positive diagonal is a quantitative measure of discriminability (assessed as the area under the curve) for which response bias has been factored out.

ROC analysis has been used extensively in basic and applied research on recognition memory. In these experiments, response bias is sometimes manipulated explicitly by encouraging observers to be more or less selective in their responses. Frequently, however, "expressed confidence level" (ECL)—the confidence that an observer holds in his or her classification—is used as a proxy for response bias, based on the assumption that more confident observers are likely to be more specific (conservative) in their responses, whereas less confident observers are likely to be less specific (liberal) in their responses.

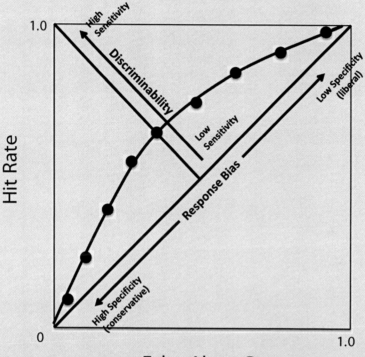

Receiver Operating Characteristic (ROC) curve.
SOURCE: Courtesy of Thomas D. Albright.

procedure over another,[42] then eyewitness performance may benefit from any procedure (such as sequential) that elicits a more conservative response bias.[43] But one can only make that judgment after having applied an empirical test to determine whether a procedure offers a discriminability advantage. Future research might explore the possibility that other methods of inducing a conservative response bias (such as verbal instructions to the witness to be cautious in making an identification) might be combined with procedures that improve discriminability in order to optimize eyewitness identification performance.

Perhaps the greatest practical benefit of recent debate over the utility of different lineup procedures is that it has opened the door to a broader consideration of methods for evaluating and enhancing eyewitness identification performance. ROC analysis is a positive and promising step with numerous advantages. For example, the area under the ROC curve is a single-number index of discriminability. Moreover, this index reflects a parameter-free approach to binary classification performance; the outcome is entirely data-dependent and thus identical across all users drawing from

---

[42]The committee notes that some of the few recent reports using ROC analysis indeed claim improved discriminability for simultaneous lineup conditions, but the reported discriminability improvements are small.

[43]In reality, a more conservative bias may not always be beneficial, and whether it is or not depends upon a number of factors that have an impact distinct from diagnostic accuracy and are difficult to quantify. All else being equal, the "best" response bias will be one that maximizes the "expected value" of the outcome (Green and Swets, *Signal Detection Theory and Psychophysics*; Swets, "ROC Analysis Applied to the Evaluation of Medical Imaging Techniques"). For the problem of eyewitness identification, the response bias that maximizes expected value can be computed from the prevalence of guilty suspects in lineups and from societal *values* or *costs* associated with each of the possible eyewitness decisions (errors and correct assignments). Reliable data on prevalence are difficult to come by, and value/cost quantities are difficult to assign and likely to vary significantly across crimes and cultures. One can nonetheless gain an intuition for how these factors might define the best response bias conditions. Consider, for example, the consequences of decreasing the prevalence of guilty suspects in lineups. In this case, expected value can be maximized by inducing a conservative bias—i.e., if innocence is a priori likely, then there is value gained by being more selective in your response. Similarly, the optimal response bias will depend upon normative costs associated with different types of eyewitness errors. Generally speaking, if a society places greater emphasis on not identifying the innocent, relative to failing to identify the guilty, then expected value can be increased by inducing a more conservative response bias. But the opposite would be true if there were greater societal pressures for identifying the guilty, relative to protecting the innocent. Although an understanding of the relationship between response bias and expected value is important, expected value in this case has little to do with the diagnostic accuracy of an eyewitness report. But it does nonetheless bear on decisions about which lineup procedure should be employed.

the same data set.[44] Most importantly for its application to the problem of evaluating eyewitness performance, the ROC approach possesses a distinct advantage because the dimensions of analysis—discriminability and response bias—map directly onto the mechanistic parameters of causal models of human recognition memory (see Chapter 4). In other words, the approach affords insight into and quantification of the sensory and cognitive processes that are believed to underlie memory-based classification decisions (see Box 5-1), such as eyewitness identifications.

Despite these merits, as a general statistical procedure for evaluation of binary classification performance and as a tool for evaluation of eyewitness performance, the ROC approach has some well-documented quantitative shortcomings. For example, ROC analysis depends on the ability to manipulate response bias or to estimate it from some other variable, and in the case of eyewitness identification that ability has been the subject of some debate. Recent studies have used expressed confidence level (ECL)—a measure of a witness' confidence in his or her selection—as a proxy for response bias,[45] based on the common-sense logic that a witness who has high confidence in their lineup selection should manifest a more conservative response bias than a witness who selected someone from the lineup despite lacking confidence in that selection (i.e., someone who made a selection even though they were not certain—a liberal response bias). This proxy relationship is inherently noisy within individuals, and the noisy relationship is exacerbated by the fact that the eyewitness identification ROC is population-based; individual data points are obtained from different people who may scale their confidence reports differently.[46] On the other hand, it is empirically clear that, when scaled appropriately (within and across individuals), different levels of expressed confidence do, in fact, correspond to different pick frequencies and response biases.[47]

---

[44] Green and Swets, *Signal Detection Theory and Psychophysics*. D. J. Hand, "Measuring Classifier Performance: A Coherent Alternative to the Area under the ROC Curve," *Machine Learning* 77, 103–123 (2009).

[45] See, e.g., N. Brewer and G. L. Wells, "The Confidence-Accuracy Relationship in Eyewitness Identification: Effects of Lineup Instructions, Foil Similarity, and Target-Absent Base Rates," *Journal of Experimental Psychology: Applied* 12(1): 11–30 (2012); Mickes, Flowe, and Wixted, "Receiver Operating Characteristic Analysis of Eyewitness Memory"; and Carlson and Carlson, "An Evaluation of Lineup Presentation."

[46] ECL is affected by over-confidence and under-confidence at the individual level, and the current implementation of the ROC approach, combining results across subjects, does not build this measurement error into the analysis or the comparison of empirical ROC curves. See Appendix C.

[47] See, e.g., Table 1 of Mickes, Flowe, and Wixted, "Receiver Operating Characteristic Analysis of Eyewitness Memory," which summarizes confidence ratings, hit rates, false alarm rates, and diagnosticity ratios (HR/FAR) derived from data published in Brewer and Wells, "The Confidence-Accuracy Relationship in Eyewitness Identification." Brewer and Wells employed

An additional prerequisite for the use of ECL as a measure of response bias is that an orderly relationship exists between confidence and accuracy—that witnesses expressing greater confidence are more likely to be accurate in their identifications. Although this hypothesis conforms to intuition,[48] the existence of a significant confidence–accuracy relationship has been challenged repeatedly over the years.[49] Recent evidence, however, suggests ways of improving the confidence–accuracy relationship (and obtaining more reliable measurements of it).[50] While the ECL measure thus has potential, more research on this and other possible methods of estimating or controlling response bias is warranted to support efforts to extract a bias-free measure of discriminability.

Another technical concern raised by the use of ROC analysis to evaluate eyewitness identification performance is that it relies on a *partial*, rather than full, area under the ROC curve measure (see Box 5-2) as an index of discriminability that is separate from response bias. This is necessitated by the fact that the highest false alarm rates in eyewitness identification data are commonly well below 1.0, even under the most liberal response bias

---

a "confidence calibration" technique to normalize scaling of expressed confidence across witnesses. Both hit rates and false alarm rates declined steeply—implying an increasingly conservative response bias—as confidence levels increased. Diagnosticity ratios increased monotonically with increasing confidence. An identical pattern can be seen in Table 3 of Mickes, Flowe, and Wixted, "Receiver Operating Characteristic Analysis of Eyewitness Memory." See also H. L. Roediger III, J. T. Wixted, and K. A. DeSoto, "The Curious Complexity Between Confidence and Accuracy in Reports from Memory," in *Memory and Law*, ed. L. Nadel and W. Sinnott-Armstrong (Oxford: Oxford University Press, 2012), 97.

[48]K. A. Deffenbacher and E. F. Loftus, "Do Jurors Share a Common Understanding Concerning Eyewitness Behavior?," *Law and Human Behavior* 6: 15–30 (1982); and G. L. Wells, T. J. Ferguson, and R. C. L. Lindsay, "The Tractability of Eyewitness Confidence and Its Implication for Triers of Fact," *Journal of Applied Psychology* 66: 688–696 (1981).

[49]G. L. Wells and D. M. Murray, "Eyewitness Confidence," in *Eyewitness Testimony: Psychological Perspectives*, ed. G. L. Wells and E. F. Loftus (New York: Cambridge University Press, 1984). B. L. Cutler and S. D. Penrod, *Mistaken Identification: The Eyewitness, Psychology, and the Law* (Cambridge: Cambridge University Press, 1995). R. K. Bothwell, K. A. Deffenbacher, and J.C. Brigham, "Correlation of Eyewitness Accuracy and Confidence: Optimality Hypothesis Revisited," *Journal of Applied Psychology* 72:691–695 (1987). S. L. Sporer et al., "Choosing, Confidence, and Accuracy: A Meta-Analysis of the Confidence-Accuracy Relation in Eyewitness Identification Studies," *Psychological Bulletin* 118(3): 315–327 (1995). T. A. Busey et al., "Accounts of the Confidence-Accuracy Relation in Recognition Memory," *Psychonomic Bulletin and Review* 7(1): 26-48 (2000).

[50]N. Brewer and G. L. Wells, "The Confidence-Accuracy Relationship in Eyewitness Identification. P. Juslin, N. Olsson, and A. Winman, "Calibration and Diagnosticity of Confidence in Eyewitness Identification: Comments on What Can Be Inferred From the Low Confidence-Accuracy Correlation," *Journal of Experimental Psychology: Learning, Memory, and Cognition* 22(5): 1304–1316 (September 1996). Roediger, Wixted, and DeSoto, "The Curious Complexity between Confidence and Accuracy." Mickes, Flowe, and Wixted, "Receiver Operating Characteristic Analysis of Eyewitness Memory."

conditions.[51] In practice, partial area under the curve is computed by truncating the ROC curve at the highest false alarm rate obtained. Because the standard error of the partial area under the curve measure depends upon the degree of truncation, accuracy of this discriminability measure can easily vary across conditions and across studies, making the interpretation difficult.[52]

While ROC analysis has many recognized merits for the evaluation of binary classification, the residual concerns associated with its typical use for evaluating eyewitness performance merit consideration of other statistical approaches to this problem. As noted above, many methods have been proposed—and adopted in specific applications—for evaluation of binary classification performance.[53] The committee knows of no instance in which any of these alternative methods has been applied to the problem of eyewitness identification. Moreover, because they have not been vetted, the committee is not in a position to endorse any specific statistical tool, the committee nevertheless encourages a general exploration of these alternatives. These alternatives may have their own share of unforeseen problems, and/or the performance criteria employed by them may bear no meaningful relationship to the sensory and cognitive processes involved in eyewitness identification. Nonetheless, some of these methods may provide greater insight into the factors that affect eyewitness identification performance and may, in turn, suggest ways of improving performance. To illustrate this opportunity by example, we consider the following possibilities.

It has been argued that a basic weakness of the existing ROC approach to binary classification performance results from the fact that, in principle

---

[51]Carlson and Carlson, "An Evaluation of Lineup Presentation." Mickes, Flowe, and Wixted, "Receiver Operating Characteristic Analysis of Eyewitness Memory."

[52]Along the same lines, accuracy of discriminability measures derived from ROC studies may be called into question when those studies do not take into account uncertainty in the data used to construct the ROC curves; see Appendix C. An argument has also been made that the area under the ROC curve can be a flawed metric for comparing binary classification conditions when the *costs* of classification errors are not precisely known and are different for different conditions (Hand, "Measuring Classifier Performance"). The costs of classification errors may be similar across some lineup comparisons and across some conditions of other systems variables, and for others they may be different. But for the most part they are not precisely known, and this is thus a topic that deserves greater attention given the growing use of ROC-based evaluation of eyewitness identification performance.

[53]Numerous methods for the evaluation of binary classifiers have been developed and applied in the field of machine learning, which seeks to optimize autonomous classification devices (such as, for example, the fingerprint lock access control on a smart phone, which must quickly and reliably distinguish the finger from another). This field has a long and rich history, and candidate methods are summarized in several texts on statistical classification and machine learning, such as Hastie, Tibshirani, and Friedman, *The Elements of Statistical Learning* and A. Smola and S. V. N. Vishwanathan, *Introduction to Machine Learning* (Cambridge: Cambridge University Press, 2009).

(and in practice under certain commonly unrecognized conditions), the area under the ROC curve is dependent on imprecise assumptions about the costs of classification errors across different classification conditions.[54] One might suppose, for example, that the cost of a miss for a crime of murder is greater than the cost of a miss for a stolen car. But without a precise understanding of these relative decision costs, the area under the ROC curve measure can be incoherent, in that it depends as much on the classification conditions as it does on the sensitivity of the classifier. An alternative method has been proposed to address this problem—derivation of the "H measure"—that enables the performance of binary classifiers to be compared using a common metric that is independent of the cost distributions for different types of classification errors.[55] The committee supports exploration of this alternative.

Another avenue for exploration emerges from the fact that the literature evaluating eyewitness identification performance has focused exclusively on the positive predictive value (PPV) of a witness' classification as guilty. For a given response bias, PPV is related to the diagnosticity ratio, in that, given equal prevalence of the culprit in two conditions (e.g., lineup procedures) being compared, a higher diagnosticity ratio leads to a higher PPV. As discussed above, the diagnosticity ratio is a critical piece of information in efforts to evaluate eyewitness performance. As for any binary classification, however, there is also information associated with a *negative* response, which is the predictive value of a classifier's assertion that a target is *not* present (in the eyewitness case, the witness' assertion of innocence). This negative predictive value (NPV) is related to a different ratio of decisions, namely $(1\text{-}HR)/(1\text{-}FAR)$,[56] in that, given equal prevalence of the target in the two procedures being compared, higher values of this ratio correspond to higher values of NPV.

While NPV is commonly used to evaluate the accuracy of human classification decisions, such as in medical diagnosis, and is a source of information that may similarly be of additional value in efforts to evaluate lineup procedures, it has been largely neglected in the field of eyewitness identification.[57] One might hold the intuition that PPV and NPV are monotonically related to one another—believing that the likelihood that the

---

[54]See Hand, "Measuring Classifier Performance."

[55]Ibid.

[56]The reciprocal of this ratio is called the "negative likelihood ratio." See, e.g., T. Hoffmann, S. Bennett, and C. del Mar, *Evidence-Based Practice Across the Health Professionals* (Chatswood: Elsevier Australia, 2009).

[57]It seems likely that this neglect stems from the fact that the primary concern in eyewitness identification has been on incorrect assertions of guilt (i.e., false identifications) rather than incorrect assertions of innocence. There are normative values in society that reinforce this concern (as exemplified, for example, by Blackstone's formulation: "Better that 10 guilty persons escape than that one innocent suffer.")

witness will correctly identify the culprit is proportional to the likelihood that the witness will correctly identify lineup candidates as innocent—and thus conclude that evaluation of PPV alone is sufficient. Contrary to that intuition, however, evidence from studies of analogous binary classification problems reveals that these two predictive probabilities can vary with respect to one another in complex ways.[58]

In practice, NPV-related measures (quantified as negative likelihood ratios) can be subjected to ROC analysis to account for the effects of response bias in the same manner as PPV-related measures (quantified as positive likelihood ratios, i.e., diagnosticity ratios)—the ROC axes in the NPV case corresponding to 1-HR and 1-FAR. Consideration of NPV and its relationship to PPV, by this and other means, may provide additional insight into the ways in which estimator and system variables (such as lineup procedures) influence eyewitness identification performance.[59]

In sum, a formal understanding of the task facing an eyewitness, in conjunction with an appreciation of causal models of human recognition memory, has led to a potentially more comprehensive method—ROC analysis—for evaluating eyewitness identification performance. Despite these advances, it is important that practitioners in this field broadly explore the large and rich field of statistical tools for evaluation of binary classifiers. While the committee recognizes that these tools are uninvestigated for this application and may possess their own share of unforeseen problems or disadvantages, a move in this direction may be of great value for improving the validity of eyewitness identification.

Interactions with Eyewitnesses (Feedback)

The nature of law enforcement interactions with the eyewitness before, during, and after the identification plays a role in the accuracy of eyewitness identifications and in the confidence expressed in the accuracy of those identifications by witnesses.[60] Law enforcement's maintenance of neutral pre-identification communications—relative to the identification of a suspect—is seen as vital to ensuring that the eyewitness is not subjected to conscious or unconscious verbal or behavioral cues that could influence the

---

[58] S-Y Shiu and C. Gatsonis, "The Predictive Receiver Operating Characteristic Curve for the Joint Assessment of the Positive and Negative Predictive Values," *Philosophical Transactions, Series A, Mathematical, Physical and Engineering Sciences* 366 (1874): 2313–2333 (2008).

[59] Another potentially informative analysis that combines PPV and NPV measures is known as a PROC (predictive ROC), which affords the opportunity to see how a given system or estimator variable may have interacting—synergistic or antagonistic—effects on assertions of guilt and innocence. See Shiu and Gatsonis, "The Predictive Receiver Operating Characteristic Curve."

[60] S. E. Clark, T. E. Marshall, and R. Rosenthal, "Lineup Administrator Influences on Eyewitness Identification Decisions," *Journal of Experimental Psychology: Applied* 15(1): 63 (2009).

eyewitness' identification (see Box 2-1).[61] If a witness happened to overhear an officer say, "We've got him, but before we finalize the arrest, let's have the witness confirm it," the witness might be biased to confirm the suspect's identity in a showup. Furthermore, some types of law enforcement communication with a witness, after the witness has made an identification (e.g., "Good work! You picked the right guy..."), can increase confidence in an identification, regardless of whether the identification is correct.[62]

As discussed in Chapter 2, use of "blinded" or "double-blind" lineup identification procedures is an effective strategy for reducing the likelihood that a witness will be exposed to cues from interactions with law enforcement (such as feedback) that could influence identifications and/ or confidence in those identifications. More generally, efforts to maintain objectivity and eliminate potentially informative communication will help ensure that eyewitness reports are not contaminated by knowledge or opinions held by others.

RESEARCH STUDIES ON ESTIMATOR VARIABLES

The impact of estimator variables on eyewitness accuracy is harder to measure in the field than the impact of system variables.[63] Consequently, estimator variables have been studied nearly exclusively in laboratory settings. The committee's review revealed the need for further empirical research in individual studies and systematic reviews of research on these factors.

The committee's review focused on the most-studied estimator variables: weapon focus, stress and fear, own-race bias, exposure, and retention interval. It is important to emphasize, however, that numerous other estimator variables may affect both the reliability and the accuracy of eyewitness identifications. Research has shown that the physical distance between the witness and the perpetrator is an important estimator variable, as it directly affects the ability of the eyewitness to discern visual details,[64] including features of the perpetrator[65] (see discussion of vision in Chapter 4). Re-

---

[61]Clark, Moreland, and Gronlund, "Evolution of the Empirical and Theoretical Foundations of Eyewitness Identification Reform": "...the performance advantage for unbiased instructions has decreased only slightly over the past 32 years. However, none of the correlations approached statistical significance." p. 258.

[62]Douglas and Steblay, "Memory Distortion in Eyewitnesses."

[63]G. L. Wells, "What Do We Know about Eyewitness Identification?" *American Psychologist* (May 1993): 553, 555.

[64]B. Uttl, P. Graf, and A. L. Siegenthaler, "Influence of Object Size on Baseline Identification, Priming, and Explicit Memory: Cognition and Neurosciences," *Scandinavian Journal of Psychology* 48(4): 281–288 (2007).

[65]C. L. Maclean et al., "Post-Identification Feedback Effects: Investigators and Evaluators," *Applied Cognitive Psychology* 25(5): 739–752 (2011).

search has also shown that an appearance change can greatly diminish the eyewitness' ability to recognize the perpetrator; the eyewitness' ability to remember faces of his or her own age group is often superior to his or her ability to remember faces of another age group (own-age bias); and if an eyewitness hears information or misinformation from another person before law enforcement involvement, his or her recollection of the event and confidence in the identification can be altered (co-witness contamination).[66] Interactions between and among these variables have not been addressed systematically by researchers.

Weapon Focus

The presence of an unusual object at the scene of a crime can impair visual perception and memory of key features of the crime event. Research suggests that the presence of a weapon at the scene of a crime captures the visual attention of the witness and impedes the ability of the witness to attend to other important features of the visual scene, such as the face of the perpetrator (see also discussion of visual attention in Chapter 4). The ensuing lack of memory of these other key features may impair recognition of a perpetrator in a subsequent lineup.

A 1992 analysis of weapon focus studies found that the presence of a weapon reduced both identification accuracy and feature accuracy (e.g., the eyewitness' ability to recall clothing, facial features, and more).[67] A more recent analysis of the weapon focus literature concluded that the presence of a weapon has an inconsistent effect on identification accuracy, in that larger effect sizes were observed in threatening scenarios than in non-threatening ones.[68] As the retention interval increased, the weapon focus effect size decreased. The analysis further indicated that the effect of a weapon on accuracy is slight in actual crimes, slightly larger in laboratory studies, and largest for simulations.

One possible cause of the inconsistent effects of the presence of a weapon is suggested by a recent laboratory-based study that exposed participants to crime videos.[69] These investigators used ROC analysis to investigate discriminability as a function of (1) sequential versus simultaneous lineups; (2) the presence of a weapon; and (3) the presence of a distinctive facial feature. Importantly for the present discussion, discriminability was

[66]R. Zajac and N. Henderson, "Don't It Make My Brown Eyes Blue: Co-Witness Misinformation about a Target's Appearance Can Impair Target-Absent Lineup Performance," *Memory* 17(3): 266–278 (2009).

[67]N. K. Steblay, "A Meta-analytic Review of the Weapon Focus Effect," *Law and Human Behavior* 16(4): 413, 415–417 (1992).

[68]Fawcett et al., "Of Guns and Geese."

[69]Carlson and Carlson, "An Evaluation of Lineup Presentation."

reduced when the perpetrator possessed a weapon, but only when no distinctive facial feature was present. This interaction between weapon focus and distinctive feature highlights the importance of exploring the effects of interactions between different estimator variables on eyewitness identification performance.

Additional questions remain as to what is the cause of reduced eyewitness performance in cases where a weapon is present. Is the effect caused by a diversion of selective attention, as is suggested by basic research on the phenomenon of inattentional blindness (see Chapter 4)? Is stress a significant factor, i.e., does anxiety cause the witness to focus less on the features of a person's face? To what extent is the prominence of the issue an artifact of the particular studies included in the meta-analysis? Is it possible, for example, that the magnitude of the weapon effect depends on whether the data are collected in a laboratory setting versus the real world? To this latter point, some analyses of weapon focus have been conducted using archival records of crimes involving weapons.[70] Unfortunately, such efforts often encounter serious methodological difficulties that include a lack of information about the crime (e.g., exposure duration) and the general lack of "ground truth" regarding accuracy of any identification, among other problems.

Stress and Fear

High levels of stress or fear can affect eyewitness identification.[71,72,73] This finding is not surprising, given the known effects of fear and stress on vision and memory (see Chapter 4). Under conditions of high stress, a witness' ability to identify key characteristics of an individual's face (e.g., hair length, hair color, eye color, shape of face, presence of facial hair) may be significantly impaired.[74]

In the particular case of weapon focus, it may not be possible to sufficiently test the effects of stress and heightened stress in the laboratory because of limitations on human participant research that uses realistic and heightened threats. A meta-analysis of the effect of high stress on eyewitness

---

[70] See, e.g., Fawcett et al., "Of Guns and Geese."

[71] Deffenbacher et al., "A Meta-Analytic Review of the Effects of High Stress."

[72] C. A. Morgan III et al., "Accuracy of Eyewitness Memory for Persons Encountered During Exposure to Highly Intense Stress," *International Journal of Law and Psychiatry* 27(3): 265–279 (2004).

[73] C. A. Morgan III et al., "Accuracy of Eyewitness Identification Is Significantly Associated with Performance on a Standardized Test of Recognition," *International Journal of Law and Psychiatry* 30 (3): 213–223 (2007).

[74] C. A. Morgan III et al., "Misinformation Can Influence Memory for Recently Experienced, Highly Stressful Events," *International Journal of Law and Psychiatry* 36(1): 11–17 (2013).

memory nonetheless found some support for the notion that stress impairs both eyewitness recall and identification accuracy.[75] The study authors noted that lineup type "moderated the effect of heightened stress on the false alarm rate."[76] They also suggested that the modest effect of stress may be caused by the fact that the analysis included many studies that involved modest stress-induction.[77]

Earlier studies were more mixed but with clearer results at "high levels of cognitive anxiety."[78] The findings of an earlier study "provide a concrete illustration of catastrophic decline" of eyewitness identification performance at high anxiety levels.[79] The correct identification rate went from 75 percent for those with low-state anxiety to 18 percent rate for those with high-state anxiety.[80]

The effects of suggestion may be particularly important when the original memory is of a highly stressful event. A recent study looked at more than 850 active-duty military personnel participating in a mock POW camp phase of U.S. military survival school training, which included aggressive interrogation and physical isolation-related stress.[81] The study found that misinformative details of the interrogation event (e.g., regarding the identity of the interrogator), which were introduced after the event had been encoded into long-term memory, affected identification accuracy. The study also found that memories acquired during stressful events are highly vulnerable to modification by exposure to post-event misinformation, even in individuals whose level of training and experience might be considered relatively immune to such influences.

Another recent study comparing the eyewitness accuracy of officers and citizens, concentrated on the effects of stress and weapon focus.[82] The results of this study showed that officers were less stressed and aroused than

---

[75]Deffenbacher et al., "A Meta-Analytic Review of the Effects Of High Stress." It should be noted that the effect sizes for stress-induced support were small with wide confidence intervals, indicating considerable heterogeneity across studies. Although the authors assert that 300 studies with null findings would be required to negate the small effects found in this meta-analysis, fewer studies might be needed if they resulted in opposite effects.

[76]Ibid, 700.

[77]Ibid, 704.

[78]Ibid, 689.

[79]T. Valentine and J. Mesout, "Eyewitness Identification Under Stress in the London Dungeon," *Applied Cognitive Psychology* 23(2): 151–161 (2009).

[80]K. A. Deffenbacher, "Estimating the Impact of Estimator Variables on Eyewitness Identification: A Fruitful Marriage of Practical Problem Solving and Psychological Theorizing," *Applied Cognitive Psychology* 22(6): 822 (2008).

[81]Morgan et al., "Misinformation Can Influence Memory."

[82]J. C. DeCarlo, "A Study Comparing the Eyewitness Accuracy of Police Officers and Citizens," (PhD Diss, City University of New York, 2010).

citizens, but that both police and citizens made more errors when a weapon was inferred or present.

Own-Race Bias

The race and ethnicity of a witness as it relates to that of the perpetrator is another important estimator variable. In eyewitness identification, own-race bias describes the phenomenon in which faces of people of races different from that of the eyewitness are harder to discriminate (and thus harder to identify accurately) than are faces of people of the same race as the eyewitness.[83] In the laboratory, this effect is manifested by higher hit rates and lower false alarm rates (higher diagnosticity ratio) in the recognition of an observer's own race relative to hits and false-alarms for recognition of other races.[84] Own-race bias occurs in both visual discrimination and memory tasks, in laboratory and field studies, and across a range of races, ethnicities, and ages. Recent analyses revealed that cross-racial (mis) identification was present in 42 percent of the cases in which an erroneous eyewitness identification was made.[85]

A recent meta-analysis of own-race bias found an interaction between own-race bias and the duration of viewing exposure: reducing the amount of time allowed for viewing of each face significantly increased the magnitude of the bias, largely manifested as an increase in the proportion of false alarm responses to other-race faces.[86] Own-race bias also interacts with the memory retention interval; cross-race errors of identification were greater when there were longer periods of time between the initial exposure and the memory retrieval.[87] A recent study found that "context reinstatement," wherein a researcher asks an individual to mentally re-create the context in which an incident occurred, failed to influence the identification of other-race faces.[88]

Although the existence of own-race bias is generally accepted, the causes for this effect are not fully understood. Some possible explanations are rooted in in-group/out-group models of human behavior (e.g., favorit-

---

[83]R. S. Malpass and J. Kravitz, "Recognition for Faces of Own and Other Race," *Journal of Personality and Social Psychology* 13(4): 330–334 (1969).

[84]Meissner and Brigham, "Thirty Years of Investigating the Own-Race Bias."

[85] The Innocence Project, "What Wrongful Convictions Teach Us About Racial Inequality," available at: http://www.innocenceproject.org/Content/What_Wrongful_Convictions_Teach_Us_About_Racial_Inequality.php.

[86]Meissner and Brigham, "Thirty Years of Investigating the Own-Race Bias."

[87]Ibid.

[88]J. R. Evans, J. L. Marcon, and C.A. Meissner, "Cross-Racial Lineup Identification: Assessing the Potential Benefits of Context Reinstatement," *Psychology, Crime, and Law* 15 (1): 19–28 (2009).

ism in which decisions regarding members of one's own "group" are regarded as having greater importance than decisions regarding members of a different "group") and differential perceptual expertise that results from different degrees of exposure to and familiarity with same versus other races.

Recent work has examined the role that stereotyping might play.[89] One study suggests that, in general, cross-race identification is further impaired when faces are presented in a group (as opposed to one at a time).[90] Additional research is needed to identify procedures that may help estimate the degree of own-race biases in individual eyewitnesses following an identification procedure. Until the scientific basis for these effects is better understood, great care may be warranted when constructing lineups in instances where the race of the suspect differs from that of the eyewitness.

Exposure Duration

Eyewitness identification researchers have long believed that exposure duration (e.g., time spent observing a perpetrator's face during a crime) is correlated with greater accuracy of eyewitness identification. The courts also have assumed that exposure duration has an effect on identification accuracy.[91] Meta-analyses on the effects of exposure time have found that relatively long exposure durations produce greater accuracy[92] and a larger and more stable effect size for exposure duration on eyewitness identi-

---

[89]H. M. Kleider, S. E. Cavrak, and L. R. Knuycky, "Looking Like a Criminal: Stereotypical Black Facial Features Promote Face Source Memory Error," *Memory and Cognition* 40(8): 1200–1213 (2012).

[90]K. Pezdek, M. O'Brien, and C. Wasson, "Cross-Race (but Not Same-Race) Face Identification Is Impaired by Presenting Faces in a Group Rather Than Individually," *Law and Human Behavior* 36(6): 488–495 (2012).

[91]*Manson v. Brathwaite*, 432 U.S. 98, 114 (1977), for example, included as a factor for assessing the reliability and admissibility of an identification, "the opportunity of the witness to view the criminal at the time of the crime" and explained that this factor includes both the length of time and the viewing conditions.

[92]B. H. Bornstein et al., "Effects of Exposure Time and Cognitive Operations on Facial Identification Accuracy: A Meta-Analysis of Two variables Associated with Initial Memory Strength," *Psychology, Crime, and Law* 18 (5): 473–490 (2012). The authors state, "We used z as the primary effect size measure for differences between proportions correct, but we also converted z to Pearson's r for comparability to other meta-analyses (see Tables 1 and 2). The rs were then normalized and averaged to obtain the overall mean effect sizes. We also report the value of Cohen's d associated with each mean effect size" (Bornstein et al., "Effects of Exposure Time and Cognitive Operations)." Although not defined, presumably z refers to the usual difference in means divided by its standard error, and, from their tables, their r was calculated as z divided by the square root of the report sample size.

fication accuracy.[93] Longer exposures were associated with higher rates of correct identifications and lower false alarm rates. Exposure duration may affect, or interact with, other variables, including own-race bias and the confidence–accuracy relationship assessed immediately after the lineup decision.[94]

The findings and conclusions from eyewitness identification studies of exposure duration are in keeping with much of the basic research on visual system function (reviewed in Chapter 4). This basic research indicates that the additional information available from longer viewing times reduces uncertainty and enables better detection and discrimination of visual stimuli.

Retention Interval

Retention interval, or the amount of time that passes from the initial observation and encoding of a memory to a future time when the initial observation must be recalled from memory, can affect identification accuracy. Laboratory studies have demonstrated that stored memories are more likely to be forgotten with the increasing passage of time and can easily become "enhanced" or distorted by events that take place during this retention interval (see discussion of memory in Chapter 4). The amount of time between viewing a crime and the subsequent identification procedure can be expected to similarly affect the accuracy of the eyewitness identification, either independently or in combination with other variables.[95]

It is difficult to specify the precise relationship between retention interval and the accuracy of eyewitness identification testimony and to estimate when a lengthy retention interval will significantly impair the accuracy of identification. Although, in general, it appears that longer retention intervals are associated with poorer eyewitness identification performance, the strength of this association appears to vary greatly across the circumstances of the initial encounter, identification procedures, and research method-

---

[93]B. H. Bornstein, K. A. Deffenbacher, E. K. McGorty, and S. D. Penrod, "The Effect of Cognitive Processing on Facial Identification Accuracy: A Meta-Analysis" (Unpublished manuscript, University of Nebraska-Lincoln, 2007).

[94]M. A. Palmer, et al., "The Confidence–Accuracy Relationship for Eyewitness Identification Decisions: Effects of Exposure Duration, Retention Interval, and Divided Attention," *Journal of Experimental Psychology: Applied* 19(1): 55–71 (2013).

[95]One month is the most commonly encountered delay by British police. G. Pike, N. Brace, and S. Kynan, *The Visual Identification of Suspects: Procedures and Practice* (London: Policing and Reducing Crime Unit, 2002), cited by Deffenbacher et al., "Forgetting the Once-Seen Face." Law enforcement authorities may have little control over the time required to identify a suspect and obtain the cooperation of the eyewitness to participate in an identification procedure. Thus, retention interval has commonly been considered an estimator variable in eyewitness identification studies.

ologies.[96] A meta-analysis of published facial recognition and eyewitness identification studies found, for example, that an increase in the retention interval was associated with a decreased probability of an accurate identification of a previously seen but otherwise unfamiliar face.[97] This same study also found that the rate of forgetting for an unfamiliar face is greatest soon after the initial observation and tends to level off over time, but was unable to specify the shape of this function.

The effect of the retention interval also is influenced by the strength and quality of the initial memory that is encoded, which, in turn, may be influenced by other estimator variables associated with witnessing the crime (such as the degree of visual attention) and viewing factors (such as distance, lighting, and exposure duration). As the retention interval becomes longer, the opportunity for intervening events to alter the memory also becomes greater, and other variables may interact with the retention interval to impair performance (see also discussion of memory in Chapter 4). During the retention interval, the ability to accurately identify faces of other races drops off especially quickly, relative to same-race accuracy.[98] Also, for those eyewitnesses who initially express less confidence in their identification, there is a greater decrease in accuracy of identification when the retention interval is longer.[99]

CONCLUSION

Research on eyewitness identification has appropriately identified the variables that may affect an individual's ability to make an accurate identification. Early research findings played an important role in alerting law enforcement, prosecutors, defense counsel, and the judiciary to factors that

---

[96]See J. Dysart and R. C. L. Lindsay, "The Effects of Delay on Eyewitness Identification Accuracy: Should We Be Concerned?" in *The Handbook of Eyewitness Psychology: Volume II: Memory for People*, ed. R. C. L. Lindsay, D. F. Ross, J. D. Read, and M. P. Toglia. (Mahwah: Lawrence Erlbaum and Associates, 2006), 361–373.

[97]Deffenbacher et al., "Forgetting the Once-Seen Face." More than 20 of the published studies included in the meta-analysis found no significant effect of retention interval.

[98]J. L. Marcon et al., "Perceptual Identification and the Cross-Race Effect," *Visual Cognition* 18(5): 767–779 (2010) (finding that the cross-race effect was more pronounced when the retention interval was lengthened). Meissner and Brigham, "Thirty Years of Investigating the Own-race Bias" [meta-analysis finding that as retention time increased "participants increasingly adopted a more liberal response criterion when responding to other-race faces. This liberal response criterion indicated that participants required less evidence from memory (e.g., familiarity or memorability of the face) to respond that they had previously seen an other-race face."].

[99]J. Sauer et al., "The Effect of Retention Interval on the Confidence–Accuracy Relationship for Eyewitness Identification," *Law and Human Behavior* 34: 337–347 (2010) (finding greater overconfidence at lengthy retention intervals).

might influence the accuracy of identifications. In some jurisdictions, eye-witness identification research was used to improve policies and procedures and to educate and train officers. However, much remains unsettled in many areas of eyewitness identification research.

While past research appropriately identified system and estimator variables that may affect an individual's ability to make an accurate identification, this research might be strengthened in several ways. Greater collaboration between the police, courts, and researchers might lead to increased consensus on research agendas and the conceptualization of variables to be examined. More attention to reproducibility and transparency is needed in the selection of data collection strategies and reporting of data. Analyses need to be reported completely, including estimates of effects, confidence intervals, and significance levels. Further, in order to be useful to stakeholders, the statistical findings of this research need to be translated back into terms that can be readily understood by practice and policy decision-makers.

Further, our understanding of errors in eyewitness identification will benefit from more effective research designs, more informative statistical measures and analyses, more probing analyses of research findings, and more sophisticated systematic reviews and meta-analyses. In view of the complexity of the effects of both system and estimator variables, and their interactions, on eyewitness identification accuracy, better experimental designs that incorporate selected combinations of these variables (e.g., presence or absence of a weapon, lighting conditions, etc.) will elucidate those variables with meaningful influence on eyewitness performance, which can inform law enforcement practice of eyewitness identification procedures. To date, the eyewitness literature has evaluated procedures mostly in terms of a single diagnosticity ratio or an ROC curve; even if uncertainty is incorporated into the analysis, many other powerful tools for evaluating a "binary classifier" are worthy of consideration.[100]

When primary studies such as those described above are available in sufficient quantities, it is important that their results are synthesized using systematic reviews that conform to current best standards.[101] These quantitative reviews would necessarily employ transparent, reproducible procedures for locating all relevant published and unpublished research; employ independent, duplicate procedures for selection of studies, extraction of data, and assessment of risk of bias; use meta-analytic procedures

---

[100]Hastie, Tibshirani, and Friedman, *The Elements of Statistical Learning*.

[101]See, e.g., A. Liberati, et al., "The PRISMA Statement for Reporting Systematic Reviews and Meta-Analyses of Studies That Evaluate Health Care Interventions: Explanation and Elaboration," *PLoS Medicine* 6(7): e1000100. doi:10.1371/journal.pmed.1000100 (2009) and Institute of Medicine, *Finding What Works in Health Care: Standards For Systematic Reviews* (Washington, DC: The National Academies Press, 2011).

that account for the heterogeneity of outcomes both within and across studies; and interpret confidence intervals around pooled effects in a way that is readily understandable by stakeholders. These systematic reviews (which would be regularly updated as new studies are conducted) can be used to further refine the research agenda in eyewitness identification research and to establish priorities for funding of additional primary research.

6

Findings and Recommendations

Eyewitnesses make mistakes. Our understanding of how to improve the accuracy of eyewitness identifications is imperfect and evolving. In the previous chapters, we described law enforcement procedures to elicit accurate eyewitness identifications; the courts' handling of eyewitness identification evidence; the science of visual perception and memory as it applies to eyewitness identifications; and the contributions of scientific research to our understanding of the variables that affect the accuracy of identifications. On the basis of its review, the committee offers its findings and recommendations for

- identifying and facilitating best practices in eyewitness procedures for the law enforcement community;
- strengthening the value of eyewitness identification evidence in court; and
- improving the scientific foundation underpinning eyewitness identification.

OVERARCHING FINDINGS

The committee is confident that the law enforcement community, while operating under considerable pressure and resource constraints, is working to improve the accuracy of eyewitness identifications. These efforts, however, have not been uniform and often fall short as a result of insufficient training, the absence of standard operating procedures, and the continuing presence of actions and statements at the crime scene and elsewhere that may intentionally or unintentionally influence eyewitness' identifications.

Basic scientific research on human visual perception and memory has provided an increasingly sophisticated understanding of how these systems work and how they place principled limits on the accuracy of eyewitness identification (see Chapter 4).[1] Basic research alone is insufficient for understanding conditions in the field and thus has been augmented by studies applied to such specific practical problem of eyewitness identification (see Chapter 5). Such applied research has identified key variables that affect the accuracy and reliability of eyewitness identifications and has been instrumental in informing law enforcement, the bar, and the judiciary of the frailties of eyewitness identification testimony.

A range of best practices has been validated by scientific methods and research and represents a starting place for efforts to improve eyewitness identification procedures. A number of law enforcement agencies have, in fact, adopted research-based best practices. This report makes actionable recommendations on, for example, the importance of adopting "blinded" eyewitness identification procedures. It further recommends that standardized and easily understood instructions be provided to eyewitnesses and calls for the careful documentation of eyewitness' confidence statements. Such improvements may be broadly implemented by law enforcement now. It is important to recognize, however, that, in certain cases, the state of scientific research on eyewitness identification is unsettled. For example, the relative superiority of competing identification procedures (i.e., simultaneous versus sequential lineups) is unresolved.

The field would benefit from collaborative research among scientists and law enforcement personnel in the identification and validation of new best practices that can improve eyewitness identification procedures. Such a foundation can be solidified through the use of more effective research designs (for example, those that consider more than one variable at a time, and in different study populations to ensure reproducibility and generalizability), more informative statistical measures and analyses (i.e., methods from statistical machine learning and signal detection theory to evaluate the performance of binary classification tasks), more probing analyses of research findings (such as analyses of consequences of data uncertainties), and more sophisticated systematic reviews and meta-analyses (that take

---

[1]Basic research on vision and memory seeks a comprehensive understanding of how these systems are organized and how they operate generally. The understanding derived from basic research includes principles that enable one to predict how a system (such as vision or memory) might behave under specific conditions (such as those associated with witnessing a crime), and to identify the conditions under which it will operate most effectively and those under which it will fail. Applied research, by contrast, empirically evaluates specific hypotheses about how a system will behave under a particular set of real-world conditions.

account of current guidelines, including transparency and reproducibility of methods).

In view of the complexity of the effects of both system and estimator variables and their interactions on eyewitness identification accuracy, better experimental designs that incorporate selected combinations of these variables (e.g., presence or absence of a weapon, lighting conditions, etc.) will elucidate those variables with meaningful influence on eyewitness performance, which can, in turn, inform law enforcement practice of eyewitness identification procedures. To date, the eyewitness literature has evaluated procedures mostly in terms of a single diagnosticity ratio or an ROC (Receiver Operating Characteristic) curve; even if uncertainty is incorporated into the analysis, many other powerful tools for evaluating a "binary classifier" are available and worthy of consideration.[2] Finally, syntheses of eyewitness research has been limited to meta-analyses that have not been conducted in the context of systematic reviews. Systematic reviews of stronger research studies need to conform to current standards and be translated into terms that are useful for decision-makers.

The committee offers the following recommendations to strengthen the effectiveness of policies and procedures used to obtain accurate eyewitness identifications.

RECOMMENDATIONS TO ESTABLISH BEST PRACTICES FOR THE LAW ENFORCEMENT COMMUNITY

The committee's review of law enforcement practices and procedures, coupled with its consideration of the scientific literature, has identified a number of areas where eyewitness identification procedures could be strengthened. The practices and procedures considered here involve acquisition of data that reflect a witness' identification and the contextual factors that bear on that identification. A recurrent theme underlying the committee's recommendations is development of, and adherence to, guidelines that are consistent with scientific standards for data collection and reporting.

Recommendation #1: Train All Law Enforcement Officers in Eyewitness Identification

The resolution and accuracy of visual perceptual experience, as well as the fidelity of our memories to events perceived, may be compromised by many factors at all stages of processing (see Chapter 4). Perceptual experiences are limited by uncertainties and biased by expectations. Unknown

---

[2]T. Hastie, R. Tibshirani, and J. H. Friedman, *The Elements of Statistical Learning: Data Mining, Inference, and Prediction* (New York: Springer, 2009).

to the individual, memories are forgotten, reconstructed, updated, and distorted. An eyewitness's memory can be contaminated by a wide variety of influences, including interaction with the police.

The committee **recommends** that all law enforcement agencies provide their officers and agents with training on vision and memory and the variables that affect them, on practices for minimizing contamination, and on effective eyewitness identification protocols. In addition to instruction at the police academy, officers should receive periodic refresher training, and officers assigned to investigative units should receive in-depth instruction. Dispatchers should be trained not to "leak" information from one caller to the next and to ask for information in a non-leading way. Police officers should be trained to ask open-ended questions, avoid suggestiveness, and efficiently manage scenes with multiple witnesses (e.g., minimize interactions among witnesses).

Recommendation #2: Implement Double-Blind Lineup and Photo Array Procedures

Decades of scientific evidence demonstrate that expectations can bias perception and judgment and that expectations can be inadvertently communicated.[3] Even when lineup administrators scrupulously avoid comments that could identify which person is the suspect, unintended body gestures, facial expressions, or other nonverbal cues have the potential to inform the witness of his or her location in the lineup or photo array.

Double-blinding is central to the scientific method because it minimizes the risk that experimenters might inadvertently bias the outcome of their research, finding only what they expected to find. For example, in medical clinical trials, double-blind designs are crucial to account for experimenter biases, interpersonal influences, and placebo effects.

To minimize inadvertent bias, double-blinding procedures are sometimes used in which the test administrator does not know the composition of the photo array or lineup. If administrators are not involved with construction of the lineup and are unaware of the placement of the potential suspect in the sequence, then they cannot influence the witness.

Some in the law enforcement community have responded to calls for double-blind lineup administration with concern, citing the potential for increased financial costs and human resource demands. The committee believes there are ways to reduce these costs and **recommends** that police departments consider procedures and new technologies that increase efficiency of data acquisition under double-blind procedures or those procedures that closely approximate double-blind procedures. If an administrator who does

---

[3]See Box 2-1.

not know the identity of the suspect cannot be assigned to the task, then a non-blind administrator (one knowing the status of the individuals in the lineup) might use a computer-automated presentation of lineup photos. If computer-based presentation technology is unavailable, then the administrator could place photos in numbered folders that are then shuffled, as is current practice in some jurisdictions.

The committee **recommends** blind (double-blind or blinded) administration of both photo arrays and live lineups and the adoption of clear, written policies and training on photo array and live lineup administration. Police should use blind procedures to avoid the unintentional or intentional exchange of information that might bias an eyewitness. The "blinded" procedure minimizes the possibility of either intentional or inadvertent suggestiveness and thus enhances the fairness of the criminal justice system. Suggestiveness during an identification procedure can result in suppression of both out-of-court and in-court identifications and thereby seriously impair the prosecutions's ability to prove its case beyond a reasonable doubt. The use of double-blind procedures will eliminate a line of cross-examination of officers in court.

Recommendation #3: Develop and Use Standardized Witness Instructions

The committee **recommends** the development of a standard set of easily understood instructions to use when engaging a witness in an identification procedure.

Witnesses should be instructed that the perpetrator may or may not be in the photo array or lineup and that the criminal investigation will continue regardless of whether the witness selects a suspect. Administrators should use witness instructions consistently in all photo arrays or lineups, and can use pre-recorded instructions or read instructions aloud, in the manner of the mandatory reading of Miranda Rights. Accommodations should be made when questioning non-English speakers or those with restricted linguistic ability. Additionally, the committee **recommends** the development and use of a standard set of instructions for use with a witness in a showup.

Recommendation #4: Document Witness Confidence Judgments

Evidence indicates that self-reported confidence at the time of trial is not a reliable predictor of eyewitness accuracy.[4] The relationship between the witness' stated confidence and accuracy of identifications may be greater at the moment of initial identification than at the time of trial. However, the strength of the confidence-accuracy relationship varies, as it depends on complex interactions among such factors as environmental conditions, persons involved, individual emotional states, and more.[5] Expressions of confidence in the courtroom often deviate substantially from a witness' initial confidence judgment, and confidence levels reported long after the initial identification can be inflated by factors other than the memory of the suspect. Thus, the committee **recommends** that law enforcement document the witness' level of confidence verbatim at the time when she or he first identifies a suspect, as confidence levels expressed at later times are subject to recall bias, enhancements stemming from opinions voiced by law enforcement, counsel and the press, and to a host of other factors that render confidence statements less reliable. During the period between the commission of a crime and the formal identification procedure, officers should avoid communications that might affect a witness' confidence level. In addition, to avoid increasing a witness' confidence, the administrator of an identification procedure should not provide feedback to a witness. Following a formal identification, the administrator should obtain level of confidence by witness' self-report (this report should be given in the witness' own words) and document this confidence statement verbatim. Accommodations should be made for non-English speakers or those with restricted linguistic ability.

Recommendation #5: Videotape the Witness Identification Process

The committee **recommends** that the video recording of eyewitness identification procedures become standard practice.

---

[4]See, e.g., C. M. Allwood, J. Knutsson, and P. A. Granhag, "Eyewitnesses Under Influence: How Feedback Affects the Realism in Confidence Judgements," *Psychology, Crime, and Law* 12(1): 25–38 (2006); B. H. Bornstein and D. J. Zickafoose, "'I Know I Know It, I Know I Saw It': The Stability of the Confidence-Accuracy Relationship Across Domain," *Journal of Experimental Psychology-Applied* 5(1): 76–88 (1999); P. A. Granhag, L. A. Stromwall, and C. M. Allwood, "Effects of Reiteration, Hindsight Bias, and Memory on Realism in Eyewitness Confidence," *Applied Cognitive Psychology* 14(5): 397–420 (2000); and H. L. Roediger III, J. T. Wixted, and K. A. DeSoto, "The Curious Complexity between Confidence and Accuracy in Reports from Memory" in *Memory and Law*, ed. L. Nadel and W. P. Sinnott-Armstrong (Oxford: Oxford University Press, 2012).
[5]See, e.g., J. M. Talarico and D. C. Rubin, "Confidence, Not Consistency, Characterizes Flashbulb Memories," *Psychological Science* 14(5): 455–461 (September 2003).

Although videotaping does have drawbacks (e.g., costs, witness advocates opposing videotaping of witnesses' faces, and witnesses not wanting to be videotaped), it is necessary to obtain and preserve a permanent record of the conditions associated with the initial identification. When necessary, efforts should be made to obtain non-intrusive recordings of the initial identification process and to accommodate non-English speakers or those with restricted linguistic ability. Measures should also be taken to protect the identity of eyewitnesses who may be at risk of harm because they make an identification.

RECOMMENDATIONS TO STRENGTHEN THE VALUE OF EYEWITNESS IDENTIFICATION EVIDENCE IN COURT

The best guidance for legal regulation of eyewitness identification evidence comes not from constitutional rulings, but from the careful use and understanding of scientific evidence to guide fact-finders and decision-makers. The *Manson v. Brathwaite* test under the Due Process Clause of the U.S. Constitution for assessing eyewitness identification evidence was established in 1977, before much applied research on eyewitness identification had been conducted. That test evaluates the "reliability" of eyewitness identifications using factors derived from prior rulings and not from empirically validated sources. As critics have pointed out, the *Manson v. Brathwaite* test includes factors that are not diagnostic of reliability. Moreover, the test treats factors such as the confidence of a witness as independent markers of reliability when, in fact, it is now well established that confidence judgments may vary over time and can be powerfully swayed by many factors. While some states have made minor changes to the due process framework, (e.g., by altering the list of acceptable "reliability" factors; see Chapter 3), wholesale reconsideration of this framework is only a recent development (e.g., the recent decisions by state supreme courts in New Jersey and Oregon; see Chapter 3).

Recommendation #6: Conduct Pretrial Judicial Inquiry

Eyewitness testimony is a type of evidence where (as with forms of forensic trace evidence) contamination may occur pre-trial. Judges rarely make pre-trial inquiries about evidence in criminal cases without one of the parties first raising an objection. In cases involving eyewitness evidence, however, parties may not be sufficiently knowledgeable about the relevant scientific research to raise concerns.

Judges have an affirmative obligation to insure the reliability of evidence presented at trial. To meet this obligation, the committee **recommends** that, as appropriate, a judge make basic inquiries when eyewitness identification evidence is offered. While the contours of such an inquiry would need to be established on a case-by-case basis, at a minimum, the judge could inquire about prior lineups, what information had been given to the eyewitness before the lineup, what instructions had been given to the eyewitness in connection with administering the lineup, and whether the lineup had been administered "blindly." The judge could also entertain requests from the parties for additional discovery and could ask the parties to brief any issues raised by these inquiries. A judge also could review reports of the eyewitness' confidence and any recordings of the identification procedures. When assessing the reliability of an identification, a judge could also inquire as to what eyewitness identification procedures the agency had in place and the degree to which they were followed. Both pre-trial judicial inquiries and any subsequent judicial review would create an incentive for agencies to adopt written eyewitness identification procedures and to document the identifications themselves.

If these initial inquiries raise issues with the identification process, a judge could conduct a pre-trial hearing to review the reliability and admissibility of eyewitness identification evidence and to assess how it should be treated at trial if found admissible. If indicia of unreliable eyewitness identifications are present, the judge should apply applicable law in deciding whether to exclude the identifications or whether some lesser sanction is appropriate. As discussed in the sections that follow, a judge may limit portions of the testimony of the eyewitness. A judge can also ensure that the jury is provided with a scientific framework within which to evaluate the evidence.

Recommendation #7: Make Juries Aware of Prior Identifications

The accepted practice of in-court eyewitness identifications can influence juries in ways that cross-examination, expert testimony, or jury instructions are unable to counter effectively. Moreover, as research suggests (see Chapters 4 and 5), the passage of time since the initial identification may mean that a courtroom identification is a less accurate reflection of an eyewitness' memory. In-court confidence statements may also be less reliable than confidence judgments made at the time of an initial out-of-court identification; as memory fails and/or confidence grows disproportionately. The confidence of an eyewitness may increase by the time of the trial as a result of learning more information about the case, participating in trial preparation, and experiencing the pressures of being placed on the stand.

An identification of the kind dealt with in this report typically should not occur for the first time in the courtroom. If no identification procedure was conducted during the investigation, a judge should consider ordering that an identification procedure be conducted before trial. In any case, whenever the eyewitness identifies a suspect in the courtroom, it is important for jurors to hear detailed information about any earlier identification, including the procedures used and the confidence expressed by the witness at that time. The descriptions of prior identifications and confidence at the time of those earlier out-of-court identifications provide more useful information to the fact-finders and decision-makers. Accordingly, the committee **recommends** that judges take all necessary steps to make juries aware of prior identifications, the manner and time frame in which they were conducted, and the confidence level expressed by the eyewitness at the time.

Recommendation #8: Use Scientific Framework Expert Testimony

The committee finds that a scientific framework describing what factors may influence a witness' visual experience of an event and the resolution and fidelity of that experience, as well as factors that underlie and influence subsequent encoding, storage, and recall of memories of an event, can inform the fact-finder in a criminal case. As discussed throughout this report, many scientifically established aspects of eyewitness memory are counterintuitive and may defy expectations. Jurors will likely need assistance in understanding the factors that may affect the accuracy of an identification. In many cases this information can be most effectively conveyed by expert testimony.

Contrary to the suggestion of some courts, the committee **recommends** that judges have the discretion to allow expert testimony on relevant precepts of eyewitness memory and identifications. Expert witnesses can explain scientific research in detail, capture the nuances of the research, and focus their testimony on the most relevant research. Expert witnesses can convey current information based on the state of the research at the time of a trial. Expert witnesses can also be cross-examined, and limitations of the research can be expressed to the jury.

Certainly, qualified experts will not be easy to locate in a given jurisdiction; and indigent defendants may not be able to afford experts absent court funds. Moreover, once the defense secures an expert, the prosecution may retain a rebuttal expert, adding complexity to the litigation. Further investigation may explore the effectiveness of expert witness presentation of relevant scientific findings compared with jury instructions. Until there is a clearer understanding of the strengths and weaknesses of this technique, the committee views expert testimony as an appropriate and effective means of providing the jury with information to assess the strength of the eyewitness identification.

Expert witnesses should not be permitted to testify without limits. An expert explaining the relevant scientific framework can describe the state of the research and focus on the factors that are particularly relevant in a given case. However, an expert must not be allowed to testify beyond the limits of his or her expertise. Although current scientific knowledge would allow an expert to inform the jury of factors bearing on their evaluation of an eyewitness' identification, the committee has seen no evidence that the scientific research has reached the point that would properly permit an expert to opine, directly or through an equivalent hypothetical question, on the accuracy of an identification by an eyewitness in a specific case.

In many jurisdictions, expert witnesses who can testify regarding eyewitness identification evidence may be unavailable. In state courts, funding for expert witnesses may be far more limited than funding in federal courts. The committee **recommends** that local jurisdictions make efforts to ensure that defendants receive funding to obtain access to qualified experts.

Recommendation #9: Use Jury Instructions as an Alternative Means to Convey Information

The committee **recommends** the use of clear and concise jury instructions as an alternative means of conveying information regarding the factors that the jury should consider.

Jury instructions should explain, in clear language, the relevant principles. Like the New Jersey instructions,[6] the instructions should allow judges to focus on factors relevant to the specific case, since not all cases implicate the same factors. Jury instructions do not need to be as detailed as the New Jersey model instructions and do not need to omit all reference to underlying research. With the exception of the New Jersey instructions, jury instructions have tended to address only certain subjects, or to repeat the problematic *Manson v. Brathwaite* language, which was not intended as instructions for jurors.

Appropriate legal organizations, together with law enforcement, prosecutors, defense counsel, and judges, should convene a body to establish model jury instructions regarding eyewitness identifications.

---

[6]New Jersey Criminal Model Jury Instructions, *Identification* (July 19, 2012), available at: http://www.judiciary.state.nj.us/pressrel/2012/jury_instruction.pdf. New Jersey Court Rule 3:11, *Record of an Out-of-Court Identification Procedure* (July 19, 2012), available at: http://www.judiciary.state.nj.us/pressrel/2012/new_rule.pdf, New Jersey Court Rule 3:13-3. *Discovery and Inspection* (July 19, 2012), available at: http://www.judiciary.state.nj.us/pressrel/2012/rev_rule.pdf.

RECOMMENDATIONS TO IMPROVE THE SCIENTIFIC FOUNDATION UNDERPINNING EYEWITNESS IDENTIFICATION RESEARCH

Basic scientific research on visual perception and memory provides important insight into the factors that can limit the fidelity of eyewitness identification (see Chapter 4). Research targeting the specific problem of eyewitness identification (see Chapter 5) complements basic scientific research. However, this strong scientific foundation remains insufficient for understanding the strengths and limitations of eyewitness identification procedures in the field. Many of the applied studies on key factors that directly affect eyewitness performance in the laboratory are not readily applicable to actual practice and policy. Applied research falls short because of a lack of reliable or standardized data from the field, a failure to include a range of practitioners in the establishment of research agendas, the use of disparate research methodologies, failure to use transparent and reproducible research procedures, and inadequate reporting of research data. The task of guiding eyewitness identification research toward the goal of evidence-based policy and practice will require collaboration in the setting of research agendas and agreement on methods for acquiring, handling, and sharing data.

Recommendation #10: Establish a National Research Initiative on Eyewitness Identification

To further our understanding of eyewitness identification, the committee **recommends** the establishment of a National Research Initiative on Eyewitness Identification (hereinafter, the Initiative). The Initiative should involve the academic research community, law enforcement community, the federal government, and philanthropic organizations. The Initiative should (1) establish a research agenda to guide research for the next decade; (2) formulate practice- and policy-relevant research questions; (3) identify opportunities for additional data collection; (4) systematically review research to examine emerging findings on the impact of system and estimator variables; (5) translate research findings into policies and procedures that are both practical and appropriate for law enforcement; and (6) set priorities and timelines for issues to be addressed, the conduct of research, the development of best practices, and formal assessments.

The committee notes that there appear to be few existing partnerships between the scientific community and law enforcement organizations and therefore **recommends** that the National Science Foundation (NSF) and the National Institute of Standards and Technology (NIST) take a leadership role working with other federal agencies, such as the National Institute of

Justice (NIJ), the Bureau of Justice Statistics (BJS), and the Federal Bureau of Investigation (FBI), to support such collaborations.

The impact on society of innocents being incarcerated while perpetrators remain free, in conjunction with limited federal resources, highlights the need for both public and private support for this Initiative.

To enhance the scientific foundation of eyewitness identification research and practice, the Initiative should commit to the following:

a. Include a **practice- and data-informed research agenda** that incorporates input from law enforcement and the courts and establishes methodological and reporting standards for research to assess the fundamental performance of various aspects of eyewitness identification procedures as well as synthesize research findings across studies.

b. Develop **protocols and policies for the collection, preservation, and exchange of field data** that can be used jointly by the scientific and law enforcement communities. Data collection procedures used in the field should be developed to ensure the relevance of the collected data, to facilitate analysis of the data, and to minimize potential bias and loss of data through incomplete recording strategies.

Law enforcement agencies should take the lead in collecting, maintaining, and sharing relevant data from the field. Much of the data that would be useful for the evaluation of eyewitness identification procedures have been collected in the form of administrative records and may be readily adapted for use in research. Comprehensive data should be collected on lineup composition and witness selections (i.e., fillers, non-identifications, and position of suspect in lineup).

c. Develop and adopt **guidelines for the conduct and reporting of applied scientific research** on eyewitness identification that conform to the highest scientific standards. All eyewitness research, including field-based studies, laboratory-based studies, and research synthesis, should use rigorous research methods and provide detailed reporting of both methods and results, including (1) pre-registration of all study protocols; (2) investigation of research questions and hypotheses informed by the needs of practice and policy; (3) adoption of strict operationalization of key measures and objective data collection; (4) development of experimental designs informed by analytical concerns; (5) use of proper statistical procedures that account for the often nontraditional nature of data in this field (e.g., estimates of effects with appropriate statements of uncertainty, multiple responses from different scenarios from the same individuals, effects of order and time of presentation when important, treatment of extreme observations or outliers); (6) reporting of participant recruitment and selection and assignment to conditions; (7) complete reporting of findings including effect sizes and associated confidence intervals for both significant and non-significant effects; and (8) derivation of conclusions that are grounded firmly in the findings of the study, are framed in the context of the strengths and limitations of study methodology, and clearly state their implications for practice and policy decisions.

Strict adherence to guidelines for eyewitness identification research will result in more credible research findings that can guide policy and practice. Research that conforms to guidelines will withstand rigorous scrutiny by peers, will be verifiable through replication, and will permit inclusion in systematic reviews, leading to greater confidence in the validity and generalizability of findings.

d. **Adopt rigorous standards for systematic reviews and meta-analytic studies.** Meta-analyses of primary studies should be conducted only in the context of systematic reviews that locate and critically appraise *all* research findings, including those from unpublished studies. Analyses should consistently appraise and account for possible biases in the included research. Studies that do not adequately conduct or report research methods, such as randomization, should be identified in the findings. Sensitivity analyses considering impacts of lower quality or inadequately reported studies on pooled effect estimates should be conducted and reported. When attempting to draw conclusions from studies with missing data, reviewers should first attempt to contact the authors of the research for additional information. When missing data cannot be retrieved from researchers, imputation methods should, if used, be specific, transparent, and reproducible. Statistical methods for meta-analysis should conform to current best practice, using models appropriate to the level of heterogeneity of results across studies, computing both point estimates and confidence intervals around effect sizes, and translating the results of meta-analyses into terms that are both understandable and useful to practice and policy decision makers.

e. **Provide basic instruction** for police, prosecutors, defense counsel, and judges on aspects of the scientific method relevant to eyewitness identifications procedures (e.g., the rationale for blinded administration), including principles of research design and the uncertainties associated with data analysis. Training should cover the importance of data collection and interpretation, including the role of standardized eyewitness identification procedures and documentation of witness statements of confidence. Competencies acquired through such training (quantitative reasoning, understanding principles of research design, and recognition of data uncertainties) are likely to apply to issues beyond eyewitness identification. For example, the knowledge and skills from training can be applied to other issues that personnel face, either in forensic science technologies or in process administration, evaluation, and quality improvement. Similarly, scientists will benefit from a greater knowledge of legal issues, standards, and procedures related to the problem of eyewitness identification. Training of both communities (law and science) will enhance communication and lead to productive collaborations.

The collaborative research initiative between researchers and law enforcement communities will be challenging as it will necessitate (1) standardized police procedures;[7] (2) systematic valid evidence collection and data entry and analysis; and (3) education and training for both researchers and law enforcement professionals on the differences between these two communities in their use of terms and considerations of standards of evidence and uncertainties in data. These three elements of a collaborative initiative are critical to advancing the science related to eyewitness identifications, as each bears directly on the integrity of the foundation upon which the efficacy and validity of current and future practices will be judged. Without such a foundation, practical advances in our scientific understanding are unlikely to occur.

The committee further **recommends** that the Initiative support research to better understand the following: (1) the variables that affect the accuracy, precision, and reliability of eyewitness identifications, and how those variables interact and vary in practice; (2) the (possibly joint) impact of estimator and system variables on both identification accuracy and response bias; (3) best practices for probing witness memory with the least potential for bias or contamination; (4) best strategies to assess witnesses' confidence levels when making an identification; (5) appropriate types of instructions for police, witnesses, and juries to best inform and facilitate the collection and interpretation of eyewitness identifications; (6) photo array composi-

---

[7]The term *standardized procedures* refers to the notion that professionals reliably follow the same set of steps or procedures. Such standardization ensures that data across cases can be considered comparable and, to a greater extent, more reliable. Although reliability is not equivalent to validity, it is essential before researchers can assess questions of validity. Without standardized procedures, valid comparisons between departments and regions of the country cannot be achieved.

tion and procedures; (7) identification procedures in the field (showups); (8) innovative technologies that might increase the reliability of eyewitness testimony (e.g., algorithm-based computer face recognition software, computer administered photo arrays, and mobile technologies with photo identification programs); and (9) the most effective means of informing jurors how to consider the factors that affect the strengths and weaknesses of eyewitness identification evidence.

Recommendation #11: Conduct Additional Research on System and Estimator Variables

Among the many variables that can affect eyewitness identification, the procedures for constructing a lineup have received the greatest attention in recent years. As discussed in Chapter 5, the question as to whether a simultaneous or sequential lineup is preferred is a specific case of the more general question of what conditions might improve the performance of an eyewitness. The answer to that question depends upon the criteria used to evaluate performance, and much of the debate has thus focused on the analysis tools for evaluation. These tools have improved significantly over the years, beginning with the use of a diagnosticity ratio, which uses the likelihood that the person identified is actually guilty as an evaluation criterion. More recently, the diagnosticity ratio approach has been augmented by analysis of Receiver Operating Characteristics (ROC analysis), which uses a measure of discriminability (i.e., a measure of how well the witness can discriminate between different possible matches to his or her memory of the face of the culprit) as an evaluation criterion. In principle, ROC analysis is a positive step, if only because it incorporates more information (i.e., the earlier diagnosticity ratio is one component of the ROC analysis). But a more complex question concerns how policy-makers and practitioners should weigh the two evaluation criteria that have been considered thus far—likelihood of guilt and discriminability—when making a decision about which lineup procedures to adopt. The answer is particularly nuanced because the two criteria do not always lead to the same conclusion; one lineup procedure may yield poorer discriminability while at the same time increasing the likelihood that the identified person is actually guilty.

The committee concludes that there should be no debate about the value of greater discriminability—to promote a lineup procedure that yields less discriminability would be akin to advocating that the lineup be performed in dim instead of bright light. For this reason, the committee **recommends** broad use of statistical tools that can render a discriminability measure to evaluate eyewitness performance. But a lineup procedure that improves discriminability can yield greater or lesser likelihood of correct identification, depending on how the procedure is applied (see Chapter 5).

For lineup procedures that yield greater discriminability, greater likelihood of correct identification would appear preferable and can be achieved by methods that elicit a more conservative response bias, such as a sequential (relative to simultaneous) lineup procedure.[8] The committee thus **recommends** a rigorous exploration of methods that can lead to more conservative responding (such as witness instructions) but do not compromise discriminability.

In view of these considerations of performance criteria and recommendations about analysis tools, can we draw definitive conclusions about which lineup procedure (sequential or simultaneous) is preferable? At this point, the answer is no. Using discriminability as a criterion, there is, as yet, not enough evidence for the advantage of one procedure over another. The committee thus **recommends** that caution and care be used when considering changes to any existing lineup procedure, until such time as there is clear evidence for the advantages of doing so. From a larger perspective, the identification of factors (such as specific lineup procedures or states of other system variables) that can objectively improve eyewitness identification performance must be among the top priorities for this field. This leads us to three additional recommendations.

a. The committee **recommends** a broad exploration of the merits of different statistical tools for use in the evaluation of eyewitness performance. ROC analysis represents an improvement over a single diagnosticity ratio, yet there are well-documented quantitative shortcomings to the ROC approach. But are there alternatives? As noted in Chapter 5, the task facing an eyewitness is a binary classification task and there exist many powerful statistical tools for evaluation of binary classification performance that are widely used, for example, in the field of machine learning. While none of these tools has been vetted for application to the problem of eyewitness identification, they offer a potentially rich resource for future investigation in this field.

b. The alternative (sequential) lineup procedure was introduced as part of an effort to improve eyewitness performance. While, as noted above, it remains unclear whether the procedure has improved eyewitness performance, that goal is still primary. In an effort to achieve that goal, many studies over the past three decades have explored the possibility that other factors may also affect performance, but until recently these investigations have not

---

[8] The committee stresses, however, that adoption of a more conservative response bias necessitates a compromise by which fewer lineup "picks" are made overall and thus fewer guilty suspects are identified (see Chapter 5).

evaluated performance using a discriminability measure. The committee therefore **recommends** a broad exploration of the effects of different system variables (e.g., additional variants on lineup procedures, witness lineup instructions) and estimator variables (e.g. presence or absence of weapon, elapsed time between incident and identification task, levels of stress) and—importantly—interactions between these variables using either the ROC approach or other tools for evaluation of binary classifiers that can be shown to have advantages over existing analytical methods.

c. Building upon the committee's call for a practice- and data-informed research agenda that incorporates input from law enforcement and the courts and establishes methodological and reporting standards for research, the committee **recommends** that the scientific community engaged in studies of eyewitness identification performance work closely with law enforcement to identify other system and estimator variables that might influence performance and practical issues that might preclude certain strategies for influencing performance. In addition, the committee **recommends** that policy decisions regarding changes in procedure should be made on the basis of evidence of superiority and should be made in consultation with police departments to determine which procedure yields the best combination of performance and practicality.

CONCLUSION

Eyewitness identification can be a powerful tool. As this report indicates, however, the malleable nature of human visual perception, memory, and confidence; the imperfect ability to recognize individuals; and policies governing law enforcement procedures can result in mistaken identifications with significant consequences. New law enforcement training protocols, standardized procedures for administering lineups, improvements in the handling of eyewitness identification in court, and better data collection and research on eyewitness identification can improve the accuracy of eyewitness identifications.

Appendixes

Appendix A

Biographical Information of Committee and Staff

CO-CHAIRS

Thomas D. Albright, Ph.D., (NAS) is Professor and Conrad T. Prebys Chair in Vision Research at the Salk Institute for Biological Studies, where he joined the faculty in 1986. Dr. Albright is also Director of the Salk Institute Center for the Neurobiology of Vision, Adjunct Professor of Psychology and Neurosciences at the University of California, San Diego, and Visiting Centenary Professor at the Indian Institute of Science, Bangalore.

Dr. Albright is an authority on the neural basis of visual perception, memory, and visually guided behavior. Probing the relationship between the activity of brain cells and perceptual state, his laboratory seeks to understand how visual perception is affected by attention, behavioral goals, and memories of previous experiences. His discoveries address the ways in which context influences visual perceptual experience and the mechanisms of visual associative memory and visual imagery. An important goal of this work is the development of therapies for blindness and perceptual impairments resulting from disease, trauma, or developmental disorders of the brain. A second aim of Dr. Albright's work is to use our growing knowledge of brain, perception, and memory to inform design in architecture and the arts, and to leverage societal decisions and public policy.

Albright received a Ph.D. in psychology and neuroscience from Princeton University in 1983. He is a recipient of numerous honors for his work, including the National Academy of Sciences Award for Initiatives in Research. Dr. Albright is a member of the National Academy of Sciences, a fellow of the American Academy of Arts and Sciences, a fellow of the

American Association for the Advancement of Science, and an associate of the Neuroscience Research Program. He is currently president of the Academy of Neuroscience for Architecture; a member of the National Academy of Sciences Committee on Science, Technology, and Law; and serves on the Scientific Advisory Committee for the Indian National Brain Research Center.

Jed S. Rakoff, J.D., has been a United States District Judge for the Southern District of New York since 1996. Prior to his appointment, he was a federal prosecutor (1973–1980) and a criminal defense lawyer at two large New York law firms (1980–1995). Judge Rakoff is coauthor of 5 books and the author of more than 110 published articles, 500 speeches, and 1,200 judicial opinions. He has been an Adjunct Professor at Columbia Law School since 1988, teaching upper class seminars in science and the law, class actions, white collar crime, and the interplay of civil and criminal law.

Judge Rakoff is a Commissioner on the National Commission on Forensic Science and is a former member of the Governance Board of the MacArthur Foundation Initiative on Law and Neuroscience. He was a member of the National Research Council Committee on the Development of the Third Edition of the Reference Manual on Scientific Evidence and the Committee on the Review of the Scientific Approaches Used During the FBI's Investigation of the 2001 *Bacillus anthracis* Mailings. He is a member of the American Academy of Arts and Sciences and the American Law Institute. He is a Judicial Fellow at the American College of Trial Lawyers, a former director of the New York Council of Defense Lawyers, and former chair of the Criminal Law Committee, New York City Bar Association.

Judge Rakoff received a B.A. from Swarthmore College in 1964, an M.Phil. from Oxford University in 1966, and a J.D. from Harvard Law School in 1969.

MEMBERS

William G. Brooks III is the Chief of the Norwood, Massachusetts Police Department. He began his tenure on May 1, 2012. He served as the Deputy Chief with the Wellesley Police Department from 2000 to 2012. As Deputy Chief, Brooks was involved in hiring, discipline, administration, budgeting, training, and multi-agency coordination. Prior to 2000, he served as a patrolman with the Westwood Police Department from 1977 to 1982 and as an officer with the Norwood Police Department from 1982 to 2000. In Norwood, he served as a patrolman and sergeant and as a detective sergeant for 14 years, supervising all criminal investigations conducted by detectives. Chief Brooks has been a police academy instructor for 30 years and a presenter on eyewitness identification for 6 years. He presents nationally on behalf of the Innocence Project, is a member of the Massachusetts Supreme Judicial Court's Study Committee on Eyewitness Identification, and was the 2012 recipient of the Innocence Network's Champion of Justice Award. Chief Brooks holds a master's degree in criminal justice and is a graduate of the FBI National Academy.

Joe S. Cecil, Ph.D., J.D, is a Project Director in the Division of Research at the Federal Judicial Center. Currently, he is directing the Center's Program on Scientific and Technical Evidence. As director, Dr. Cecil is responsible for judicial education and training in the area of scientific and technical evidence and served as principal editor of the first two editions of the Center's *Reference Manual on Scientific Evidence,* which is the primary source book on evidence for federal judges. He also has published several articles on the use of court-appointed experts. Dr. Cecil is currently directing a research project that examines the difficulties that arise with expert testimony in federal courts, with an emphasis on clinical medical testimony and forensic science evidence. Other areas of research interest include federal civil and appellate procedure, jury competence in complex civil litigation, and assessment of rule of law in emerging democracies. Dr. Cecil serves on the editorial boards of social science and legal journals. He previously served on the National Academies' Panel on Confidentiality and Data Access and the Committee on Identifying the Needs of the Forensic Sciences Community. He currently is a member of the National Academy of Sciences' Committee on Science, Technology, and Law and was a member of its Access to Research Data: Balancing Risks and Opportunities subcommittee. Dr. Cecil received his doctorate (in psychology) and law degree from Northwestern University.

Winrich Freiwald, Ph.D., is Assistant Professor, Laboratory of Neural Systems, The Rockefeller University. Dr. Freiwald is interested in the neural processes that form object representations as well as those that allow attention to make those representations available for social behavior and cognition. Dr. Freiwald co-discovered a specialized neural machinery for face processing located in the temporal and frontal lobes of the brain. He and his colleagues further showed that this machinery is composed of a small network of a fixed number of face selective regions, termed face patches, each dedicated to a different aspect of face processing and all closely connected with each other. Dr. Freiwald's laboratory aims to understand the inner workings of this system, from the level of individual cells to the interactions of brain areas, in order to answer questions such as: How does face selectivity emerge in a single cell? How is information transformed from one face patch to another? What is the contribution of each face patch to different face recognition abilities like the recognition of a friend or a smile? How do the different face patches interact in different tasks? And how is information extracted from a patch when a perceptual decision is made?

Dr. Freiwald, a native of Oldenburg, Germany, performed his graduate work at the Max Planck Institute for Brain Research in Frankfurt and received his Ph.D. from Tübingen University in 1998. He then joined the Institute for Brain Research at the University of Bremen as a lecturer. Starting in 2001, he worked as a postdoctoral fellow at the Massachusetts Institute of Technology, Massachusetts General Hospital, Harvard Medical School, and the Hanse Institute for Advanced Study in Delmenhorst, Germany. He was head of the primate brain imaging group at the Centers for Advanced Imaging and Cognitive Sciences in Bremen from 2004 to 2008 and a visiting associate at the California Institute of Technology in 2009. He joined The Rockefeller University as assistant professor in 2009. Dr. Freiwald was named a Pew Scholar in 2010, a McKnight Scholar in 2011, and a NYSCF—Robertson Neuroscience Investigator in 2013.

Brandon L. Garrett is the Roy L. and Rosamond Woodruff Morgan Professor of Law at the University of Virginia Law School. Garrett joined the law faculty in 2005. His research and teaching interests include criminal procedure, wrongful convictions, habeas corpus, corporate crime, scientific evidence, civil rights, civil procedure, and constitutional law.

Mr. Garrett's recent research includes studies of DNA exonerations, organizational prosecutions, and eyewitness identification procedures in Virginia. In 2011, Harvard University Press published Mr. Garrett's book, *Convicting the Innocent: Where Criminal Prosecutions Go Wrong*, examining the cases of the first 250 people to be exonerated by DNA testing. In 2013, Foundation Press published his co-authored casebook, *Federal Habeas Corpus: Executive Detention and Post-Conviction Litigation*. Mr. Garrett is currently completing a new book, in contract with Harvard University Press, examining corporate prosecutions.

Mr. Garrett attended Columbia Law School, where he was an articles editor of the *Columbia Law Review* and a Kent Scholar. After graduating, he clerked for the Honorable Pierre N. Leval of the United States Court of Appeals for the Second Circuit. He then worked as an associate at Neufeld, Scheck & Brustin LLP in New York City.

Karen Kafadar, Ph.D., is Commonwealth Professor and Chair of Statistics at the University of Virginia. Dr. Kafadar received her B.S. in mathematics and M.S. in statistics at Stanford University and her Ph.D. in statistics from Princeton University. Before joining the Statistics Department in 2014, she was Mathematical Statistician at the National Institute of Standards and Technology, member of the technical staff at Hewlett Packard's

RF/Microwave R&D Department, Fellow in the Division of Cancer Prevention at National Cancer Institute, Professor and Chancellor's Scholar at University of Colorado-Denver, and Rudy Professor of Statistics at Indiana University-Bloomington. Her research focuses on robust methods, exploratory data analysis, characterization of uncertainty in the physical, chemical, biological, and engineering sciences, and methodology for the analysis of screening trials, with awards from CDC, American Statistical Association (ASA), and American Society for Quality.

Kafadar was editor of *Technometrics* and the review section of the *Journal of the American Statistical Association* and is currently Biology, Medicine, and Genetics Editor for *The Annals for Applied Statistics*. She has served on several National Research Council committees and is a past or present member on the governing boards for ASA, Institute of Mathematical Statistics, International Statistical Institute, and National Institute of Statistical Sciences. She is a Fellow of the ASA, the American Association for the Advancement of Science, and the International Statistics Institute; she has authored more than 100 journal articles and book chapters; and has advised numerous M.S. and Ph.D. students.

A.J. Kramer, J.D., is Federal Public Defender for the District of Columbia. He earned a Bachelor's of Arts from Stanford University (1975), followed by a Juris Doctorate from the Boalt Hall School of Law at the University of California at Berkeley (1979). Mr. Kramer clerked for the Honorable Procter Hug, Jr., at the United States Court of Appeals for the Ninth Circuit in Reno, Nevada. He spent seven years as an Assistant Federal Public Defender in San Francisco, California, followed by three years as the Chief Assistant Federal Public Defender in Sacramento, California. He taught legal research and writing at Hastings College of the Law, University of California, San Francisco from 1982 to 1988. Mr. Kramer was appointed Federal Public Defender for the District of Columbia in 1990.

A permanent faculty member at the National Criminal Defense College in Macon, Georgia, and at the Western Trial Advocacy Institute in Laramie, Wyoming, Mr. Kramer is a Fellow of the American College of Trial Lawyers. He is currently a member of the American Bar Association Criminal Justice Section Council and a member of the United States Judicial Conference Advisory Committee on the Rules of Evidence.

Scott McNamara, J.D., graduated from Syracuse University with a major in mathematics. Mr. McNamara attended Vermont Law School, graduating *cum laude* in 1991. On July 20, 1992, he became an Oneida County Assistant District Attorney. As such, he handled thousands of cases with a concentration in narcotic and homicide prosecutions. McNamara was the Bureau Chief of the Narcotics Unit for twelve years, and he was also the First Assistant District Attorney for six years. During his years in the District Attorney's Office, he was a member and the lead prosecutor assigned to the Oneida County Drug Task Force. He also chaired the Oneida County District Attorney's Office Death Penalty Committee. From 2001 to 2006, Mr. McNamara represented the District Attorney's Office on the Joint Terrorism Task Force. In January of 2007, Mr. McNamara took office as the Oneida County District Attorney and has since been elected, and re-elected, by the citizens of Oneida County. His tenure as District Attorney has been one of proactive engagement and problem-solving. He has created an Economic Crime Unit, a Conviction Integrity Unit, and he has appointed a community liaison to improve communication and accessibility between the District Attorney's Office and the diverse population it serves. In addition, Mr. McNamara initiated a strategy of video recording all police interrogations in Oneida County. He has always maintained that his goal as the county's chief law enforcement officer is to continue the legacy of bringing justice to those victimized by crime while recognizing the need to safeguard and enhance fairness within the legal system.

For 10 years, Mr. McNamara taught search and seizure at the Mohawk Valley Police Academy. He was also an adjunct instructor at Mohawk Valley Community College, where he taught both criminal law and constitutional criminal procedural law. McNamara currently is an adjunct instructor at Utica College, where he teaches legal concepts of criminal fraud.

Charles Alexander Morgan III, M.D., is Associate Clinical Professor of Psychiatry, Yale University School of Medicine. Over the course of twenty years at Yale University and the Neurobiological Studies Unit of National Center for Posttraumatic Stress Disorder, Dr. Morgan's neurobiological and forensic research has established him as an international expert in posttraumatic stress disorder (PTSD), in eyewitness memory, and in human performance under conditions of high stress. He is a forensic psychiatrist and has testified as an expert on memory and PTSD at the International Tribunal on War Crimes, the Hague, Netherlands. Dr. Morgan is subject matter expert in the selection and assessment of U.S. Military Special Operations and Special Mission Units. His work has provided insight into the psycho-neurobiology of resilience in elite soldiers and has contributed to the training mission of U.S. Army special programs. For his work in the special operations community, Dr. Morgan was awarded the U.S. Army Award for Patriotic Service in 2008. In 2010, Dr. Morgan was awarded the Sir Henry Welcome Medal and Prize for his research on enhancing cognitive performance under stress in special operations personnel. In 2011, Dr. Morgan deployed to Afghanistan as an operational advisor with the Asymmetric Warfare Group.

Elizabeth A. Phelps, Ph.D., is Silver Professor of Psychology and Neural Science at New York University. Her research examines the cognitive neuroscience of emotion, learning, and memory. Her primary focus has been to understand how human learning and memory are changed by emotion and to investigate the neural systems mediating their interactions. She has approached this topic from a number of different perspectives, with an aim of achieving a more global understanding of the complex relations between emotion and memory. As much as possible, Dr. Phelps has tried to let the questions drive the research, not the techniques or traditional definitions of research areas. Dr. Phelps has used a number of techniques (behavioral studies, physiological measurements, brain-lesion studies, fMRI) and has collaborated with a number of people in other domains (social and clinical psychologists, psychiatrists, neuroscientists, economists, physicists). Dr. Phelps received a Ph.D. in neuroscience from Princeton University.

Daniel J. Simons, Ph.D., is a professor in the department of psychology at the University of Illinois, where he heads the Visual Cognition Laboratory. His research explores the limits of awareness and memory, the reasons why we often are unaware of those limits, and the implications of such limits for our personal and professional lives. He is best known for his research that demonstrates how people are far less aware of their visual surroundings than they think.

Dr. Simons received his B.A. from Carleton College and his Ph.D. in experimental psychology from Cornell University. He then spent 5 years on the faculty at Harvard University before being recruited to Illinois in 2002. He has published more than 50 articles for professional journals, and his work has been supported by the National Institutes of Health, the National Science Foundation, and the Office of Naval Research. He is a Fellow and Charter Member of the Association for Psychological Science and an Alfred P. Sloan Fellow, and he has received many awards for his research and teaching, including the 2003 Early Career Award from the American Psychological Association. His research adopts methods ranging from real-world and video-based approaches to computer-based psychophysical techniques, and it includes basic behavioral measures, survey and individual difference methods, simulator studies, and training studies. This diversity of approaches helps establish closer links between basic research on the mechanisms of attention, perception, memory, and awareness and how those mechanisms operate in the real world.

In addition to his scholarly research, Dr. Simons is the co-author (with Christopher Chabris) of the *New York Times* bestselling book, *The Invisible Gorilla*. He has penned articles for the *New York Times*, the *Wall Street Journal*, the *Los Angeles Times*, and the *Chicago Tribune* (among others), and he appears regularly on radio and television.

Anthony D. Wagner, Ph.D., is a Professor of Psychology and Neuroscience and Co-Director, Center for Cognitive and Neurobiological Imaging, Stanford University. He is also Director of the Stanford Memory Laboratory. At Stanford since 2003, Dr. Wagner's research explores how the brain supports learning, memory, and executive function. In addition to his basic science, his research examines memory dysfunction in clinical populations and the role of neuroscience evidence in legal and educational settings. He is on the faculty in the Psychology Department and participates in the Neurosciences Program, the Symbolic Systems Program, the Human Biology Program, and the Stanford Center for Longevity. Externally, he is a member of the MacArthur Foundation's Research Network on Law and Neuroscience. He is a Fellow of the American Association for the Advancement of Science, and a recipient of the American Psychological Association's Distinguished Scientific Award for Early Career Contribution, among other honors. Dr. Wagner received a Ph.D. in psychology from Stanford University in 1997.

Joanne Yaffe, Ph.D., is Professor, College of Social Work, University of Utah and Adjunct Professor of Psychiatry, College of Medicine, University of Utah. Her scholarly interests are in evidence based practice and using scientific knowledge for policy and practice decisions. She is particularly interested in the synthesis of research through systematic reviews and meta-analysis, and, with colleagues in the United Kingdom, was funded by the Cochrane Collaboration to develop guidelines for reporting systematic reviews without included studies. She is affiliated with the Social Welfare Coordinating Group and the Knowledge Translation Group of the Campbell Collaboration and has worked with the Methods Group of the Cochrane Collaboration. Dr. Yaffe is a member of the International Advisory Group for CONSORT-SPI, which has developed guidelines for the reporting of randomized trials for complex social and psychological interventions. Dr. Yaffe received a B.S. in Psychology from University of Massachusetts, an M.S.W. from the University of Michigan, and a Ph.D. in Social Work and Psychology from the University of Michigan. She has advanced training in systematic reviews and meta-analysis.

STAFF

Anne-Marie Mazza, Ph.D., is the Director of the Committee on Science, Technology, and Law. Dr. Mazza joined the National Academies in 1995. She has served as Senior Program Officer with both the Committee on Science, Engineering and Public Policy and the Government-University-Industry Research Roundtable. In 1999, she was named the first director of the Committee on Science, Technology, and Law, a newly created activity designed to foster communication and analysis among scientists, engineers, and members of the legal community. Dr. Mazza has been the study director on numerous Academy reports including, *Reference Manual on Scientific Evidence*, 3rd Edition (2011); *Review of the Scientific Approaches Used During the FBI's Investigation of the 2001 Anthrax Letters* (2011); *Managing University Intellectual Property in the Public Interest* (2010); *Strengthening Forensic Science in the United States: A Path Forward* (2009); *Science and Security in A Post 9/11 World* (2007); *Reaping the Benefits of Genomic and Proteomic Research: Intellectual Property Rights, Innovation, and Public Health* (2005); and *Intentional Human Dosing Studies for EPA Regulatory Purposes: Scientific and Ethical Issues* (2004). Between October 1999 and October 2000, Dr. Mazza divided her time between the National Academies and the White House Office of Science and Technology Policy, where she served as a Senior Policy Analyst responsible for issues associated with a Presidential Review Directive on the government-university research partnership. Before joining the Academy, Dr. Mazza was a Senior Consultant with Resource Planning Corporation. She is a fellow of the American Association for the Advancement of Science. Dr. Mazza was awarded a B.A., M.A., and Ph.D. from The George Washington University.

Arlene F. Lee, J.D., is the Board Director for the Committee on Law and Justice (CLAJ). Prior to joining CLAJ, Ms. Lee was the Director of Policy at the Center for the Study of Social Policy, where she focused on helping federal and state elected officials develop research-informed policies and funding to improve results for children and families. In this capacity, she oversaw PolicyforResults.org, a leading national resource for results-based policy. Previously she was the Executive Director of the Maryland Governor's Office for Children, where she chaired the Children's Cabinet and was responsible for the cabinet's fund of 60+ million dollars annually. She has served as the Deputy Director of the Georgetown University Center for Juvenile Justice Reform, Director of the Federal Resource Center for Children of Prisoners, and Youth Strategies Manager for the Governor's Office of Crime Control and Prevention. Ms. Lee is also the author of numerous articles and coauthored *The Impact of the Adoption and Safe Families Act on Children of Incarcerated Parents*. She has a B.A. in Sociology from Washington College and a J.D. from Washington College of Law, American University. As a result of her work, Ms. Lee was named one of Maryland's Top 100 Women and has received three Governor's Citations.

Steven Kendall, Ph.D., is Program Officer for the Committee on Science, Technology, and Law. Dr. Kendall has contributed to numerous Academy reports including the *Reference Manual on Scientific Evidence*, 3rd Edition (2011); *Review of the Scientific Approaches Used During the FBI's Inves-*

tigation of the 2001 Anthrax Mailings (2011); *Managing University Intellectual Property in the Public Interest* (2010); and *Strengthening Forensic Science in the United States: A Path Forward* (2009). Dr. Kendall received his Ph.D. from the Department of the History of Art and Architecture at the University of California, Santa Barbara, where he wrote a dissertation on 19th century British painting. He received his M.A. in Victorian Art and Architecture at the University of London. Prior to joining the National Research Council in 2007, Dr. Kendall worked at the Smithsonian American Art Museum and The Huntington in San Marino, California.

Karolina Konarzewska is Program Coordinator for the Committee on Science, Technology, and Law. Ms. Konzarzewska received a B.A. in Political Science from the College of Staten Island, City University of New York and an M.A. in International Relations, New York University. Prior to joining The National Academies, she worked at various research institutions in Washington, DC, where she covered political and economic issues pertaining to Europe, Russia, and Eurasia.

Appendix B

Committee Meeting Agendas

Meeting 1
Washington, DC
Monday, 2 December 2013

OPEN SESSION

8:00   Continental Breakfast

8:30   Opening Remarks and Introductions

                Co-chairs:

                Thomas D. Albright, Salk Institute for Biological Studies
                Jed S. Rakoff, U.S. District Court for the Southern District
                of New York

8:45–9:30   Charge to the Committee

                Speaker:

                Anne Milgram, Laura and John Arnold Foundation

9:30–11:00   The Science of Memory—A Dynamic Process

Speakers:

Daniel L. Schacter, Harvard University (via videoconference)
John T. Wixted, University of California, San Diego

11:00–11:15   Break

11:15–12:00   Overview of Eyewitness Identification

Speaker:

Gary L. Wells, Iowa State University

12:00–1:00   Lunch

1:00–2:30   Meta-Analytical Reviews of System and Estimator Variables

Speakers:

Nancy K. Steblay, Augsburg College
Christian A. Meissner, Iowa State University
Kenneth Deffenbacher, University of Nebraska at Omaha

2:30–3:00   Strengths and Weaknesses of Eyewitness Research Methodologies

Speaker:

Steven D. Penrod, John Jay College of Criminal Justice

3:00–3:30   General Acceptance of Eyewitness Testimony Research

Speaker:

Saul Kassin, John Jay College of Criminal Justice

3:30–3:45   Break

3:45–4:15   Simultaneous and Sequential Lineups

Speaker:

Roy S. Malpass, University of Texas at El Paso

4:15–5:15   Perspectives on Eyewitness Identification

Speakers:

John Firman, International Association of Chiefs of Police
David LaBahn, Association of Prosecuting Attorneys
Kristine Hamann, National District Attorney's Association
Barry Scheck, The Innocence Project

Tuesday, 3 December 2013

CLOSED SESSION: 8:00–9:15

OPEN SESSION

9:30–10:15   Police Practices

Speakers:

Joseph Salemme, Chicago Police Department
Rob Davis, Police Executive Research Forum

10:15–11:45 Judicial Findings and Recommendations—Including Jury
Instructions

Speakers:

The Honorable Robert J. Kane, Supreme Judicial Study
Group on Eyewitness Identification (MA)
The Honorable Geoffrey Gaulkin, Special Master, *State v. Henderson* (NJ)
The Honorable Paul De Muniz, Oregon Supreme Court
The Honorable Barbara Hervey, Texas Court of Criminal
Appeals

11:45–12:30   Research on Jury Instructions

Speakers:

Shari Seidman Diamond, Northwestern University and
American Bar Foundation
David V. Yokum, University of Arizona

CLOSED SESSION: 12:30–2:00

Meeting 2
Washington, DC
Thursday, 6 February 2014

OPEN SESSION

8:30–8:45   Opening Remarks and Introductions

Co-chairs:

Thomas D. Albright, Salk Institute for Biological Studies
Jed S. Rakoff, U.S. District Court for the Southern District
of New York

8:45–9:30   The Illinois Pilot Program on Sequential Double-Blind
Identification Procedures

Speaker:

Sheri Mecklenburg, U.S. Department of Justice

9:30–10:15   Face Recognition and Human Identification

Speaker:

P. Jonathon Phillips, National Institute of Standards and
Technology

10:15–10:30   Break

10:30–11:15   Evaluating Eyewitness Research in Court: Moving from General to Specific Inference

Speaker:

John Monahan, University of Virginia

11:15–12:00   Eyewitness Identification from the Perspective of State Attorney Generals

Speaker:

Peter Kilmartin, State of Rhode Island

12:00–12:45   Lunch

12:45–1:30   Costs and Benefits of Eyewitness Identification Reforms

Speaker:

Steven E. Clark, University of California, Riverside

1:30–2:30   Misinformation and the Creation of False Memories

Speaker:

Elizabeth Loftus, University of California, Irvine—via videoconference

2:30–3:15   Obtaining Better Descriptive Information: The Use of the Cognitive Interview

Speaker:

Ronald Fisher, Florida International University

CLOSED SESSION: 3:30–5:30

Friday, 7 February 2014

CLOSED SESSION: 8:00–2:00

Meeting 3
Washington, DC
Thursday, 24 April 2014

OPEN SESSION

10:30   Welcome

               Co-chairs:

               Thomas D. Albright, Salk Institute for Biological Studies
               Jed S. Rakoff, U.S. District Court for the Southern District
               of New York

10:35–11:30   Photo Arrays in Eyewitness Identification Procedures

               Speaker:

               Karen L. Amendola, Police Foundation

CLOSED SESSION: 11:45–5:00

Friday, 25 April 2014

CLOSED SESSION: 8:30–3:00

Appendix C

Consideration of Uncertainty in Data on the Confidence-Accuracy Relationship and the Receiver Operating Characteristic (ROC) Curve

What has happened is history. What might have happened is science and technology. So what you are really interested in is what might have happened if you could do it all over again.

John W. Tukey, 18 November 1992, in a
discussion of assessing the uncertainty in cancer
mortality rates at the National Cancer Institute

Both the Receiver Operating Characteristic (ROC) and the confidence–accuracy relationship involve data (usually, as the proportions of participants in a given study that meet some criterion) and hence are subject to various sources of uncertainty, including measurement error, random variations from external conditions, and biases (such as the tendency to respond "conservatively" or "liberally"; see examples of these biases in Chapter 5). Appendix C focuses on quantification of uncertainty in some of the errors caused by measurement and other random sources. Because the confidence-based ROC curve is justified by an implicit assumption that confidence and accuracy are related, the first section of this appendix discusses the incorporation of uncertainty when assessing the strength of the confidence–accuracy relationship, and the second section does the same for the ROC curve. In what follows, *HR* denotes the hit rate (or "sensitivity" of a procedure on which the confidence–accuracy relationship or ROC is being constructed), and *FAR* (or, 1 – specificity; see Chapter 5) denotes the false alarm rate.[1]

CONFIDENCE–ACCURACY RELATIONSHIP

When authors talk about the confidence–accuracy relationship, they usually are referring to a correlation coefficient or to a slope of the line fitted to the points (C, A), where a measure of the eyewitness' expressed confidence level C is on the x-axis, and a measure of the witnesses's accuracy A is on the y-axis. However one measures the significance of the confidence–accuracy relationship (e.g., in either a correlation coefficient or a slope of the line fitted to the [C, A] points), it is important to note that both expressed confidence level (C) and reported accuracy (A) are based on data and thus are subject to uncertainty, both from random and systematic sources of variation and from biases (see, e.g., Chapter 5 for examples of biases and other variables, such as the type of lineup procedure). In this appendix, we consider the effects of uncertainty in only "A" and "C" in assessing the strength of the confidence–accuracy relationship. Ideally, one would repeat the incident multiple times and assess the error in the repetitions. Unfortunately, such repetition is usually not possible, and one must rely on approximate measures of uncertainty with regard to the (C, A) points. Approaches for characterizing the uncertainty in the confidence–accuracy relationship, using data in the published literature, follow.

Consider the following data:[2]

1) $n_1 = 44$ participants who expressed "Low" confidence (confidence ratings 1,2,3); their overall accuracy was stated as 61%. Taking the median of these three confidence ratings, $C_1 = 2$ and $A_1 = 0.61$. The estimated standard error of this proportion is $(0.61 \cdot 0.39/44)^{1/2} = 0.0735$.

---

[1]The data cited here are used for convenience, as the source publications provided sufficient details about the illustrations.

[2]These data are cited in H. L. Roediger III, J. T. Wixted, and K. A. DeSoto. "The Curious Complexity Between Confidence and Accuracy in Reports from Memory" in *Memory and Law*, ed. L. Nadel and W. P. Sinnott-Armstrong (Oxford: Oxford University Press, 2012), p. 109, who in turn cite Odinot, Wolters, and van Koppen [G. Odinot, G.Wolters, and P. J. van Koppen, "Eyewitness Memory of a Supermarket Robbery: A Case Study of Accuracy And Confidence after 3 Months," *Law and Human Behavior* 33: 506–514 (2009)] as the source of these data, from nine "central witnesses" (five other witnesses were not interviewed by the police). The sample sizes (44, 203, 326) apparently arise from having "averaged across different categories (person descriptions, object descriptions, and action details) for the nine central witnesses interviewed in that study"; see J. T. Wixted et al., "Confidence Judgments Are Useful in Eyewitness Identifications: A New Perspective," submitted to *Applied Psychology* 2014, p. 17.

2) n_2 = 203 participants who expressed "Medium" confidence (confidence ratings 4,5,6); their overall accuracy was stated as 71%. Taking the median of these three confidence ratings, C_2 = 5 and A_2 = 0.71. The estimated standard error of this proportion is $(0.71 \cdot 0.29/203)^{1/2}$ = 0.0318.

3) n_3 = 326 participants who expressed "High" confidence (confidence rating 7); their overall accuracy was stated as 85%. Thus, C_3 = 7 and A_3 = 0.85. The estimated standard error of this proportion is $(0.85 \cdot 0.15/326)^{1/2}$ = 0.0198.

A plot of these three data points might suggest a highly convincing relationship between accuracy and confidence. However, the relationship is not "statistically significant" when assessed via a weighted linear regression (where weights are inversely proportional to either the standard errors or the variances), nor via an unweighted Pearson correlation coefficient or a Spearman's rank correlation coefficient (which depends less on the assignment of "Low," "Medium," and "High" as 2, 5, 7, respectively, than do the other two methods). Separate tests comparing the proportions 0.85 ("High") versus either 0.71 ("Medium") or 0.61 ("Low") are "statistically significant," but not the test for comparing the proportions 0.71 ("Medium") and 0.61 ("Low"). Statistical significance is difficult to achieve with only three data points. Moreover, none of these tests takes into account the potential for error in the self-reported "C" values (2,5,7), which, as discussed in the previous paragraph, is likely to exist.

Consider a second set of data, reported in Juslin, Olsson, and Winman.[3] In this article, the authors considered two lineup conditions, denoted as "suspect-similarity" and "culprit-description." The authors correctly note that the identification rates at each expressed confidence level for these two conditions are very similar; hence, as the condition had no effect on identification accuracy, one might as well pool "successes/trials" across the two conditions to reduce the uncertainty in each of the accuracy rates and thus gain greater power.

Even after combining the two conditions, however, the numbers of trials in the 10 ECL categories (0.1 = "10% confident," 0.2 = "20% confident" ... 1.0 = "100% confident") are not very high (the 10 numbers range from 7 for ECL = 20% to 45 for ECL = 90%). To increase the chances of seeing a meaningful relationship between confidence and accuracy, the authors pool 0.1 with 0.2, 0.3 with 0.4, 0.5 with 0.6, 0.7 with 0.8, and 0.9 with

[3]P. Juslin, N. Olsson, and A. Winman, "Calibration and Diagnosticity of Confidence in Eyewitness Identification: Comments on What Can Be Inferred from the Low Confidence-Accuracy Correlation," *Journal of Experimental Psychology: Learning, Memory, and Cognition* 22(5): 1304–1316 (September 1996).

1.0. Although Table 2 in Juslin, Olsson, and Winman provides the counts (numbers of trials), it does not tabulate the accuracies (numbers of correct responses). One can estimate these accuracies by weighted averages of the displayed percentages shown in the plots in their Figure 2[4] for the "suspect-similarity condition" ("A" = 0.27, 0.38, 0.51, 0.55, 0.87; n = 15, 21, 25, 29, 51) and for the "culprit-description condition" ("A" = 0.18, 0.66, 0.63, 0.90, 0.91; n = 10, 18, 28, 41, 37). In the confidence level categories (15%, 35%, 55%, 75%, 95%), the accuracies (with their standard errors and the total sample sizes on which they are based following them in parentheses) are, respectively, 23.4% (8.5%, n = 25), 50.9% (8.0%, n = 39), 52.6% (6.9%, n = 53), 75.5% (5.1%, n = 70), and 88.7% (3.4%, n = 88). For these data, both the unweighted correlation coefficient, 0.9766 (t-statistic = 7.865, p-value 0.004), and the slope of the weighted linear regression (points weighted inversely proportional to their standard errors), 0.773 (standard error 0.085, p-value 0.003), are statistically significant, in that such convincing data of a relationship between correlation and accuracy would be unlikely to arise if, in fact, no association existed.

Another method for assessing the significance of the unweighted correlation is through the simulation of a large number of trials on the basis of the data that were observed. For each trial, one can first simulate five confidence values, uniformly distributed between the endpoints that were observed: c_1 is uniformly distributed between (0.05, 0.25) (mean is the observed 0.15); c_2 is uniformly distributed between (0.25, 0.45) (mean is the observed 0.35); ... c_5 is uniformly distributed between (0.85, 1.00). Next, one simulates five proportions using the observed conditions: a_1 is a binomial variate (n = 25, p = 0.234) divided by n = 25; a_2 is a binomial variate (n = 39, p = 0.509) divided by n = 39; ... a_5 is a binomial variate (n = 88, p = 0.887) divided by n = 88. For each trial with five simulated c values and their five corresponding a values, one calculates a Pearson correlation coefficient. Figure C-1 shows a plot of the five data points, with limits of one standard error on the estimated accuracies (left panel) and the histogram of the 1,000 simulated Pearson correlation coefficients (right panel). The median is 0.9534 (close to the observed 0.9766), the upper and lower quartiles are 0.916 and 0.977, and the central 90% of the 1,000 values lie between 0.8650 and 0.993. Thus, an approximate 90% confidence interval for the true correlation coefficient (0.865, 0.993) definitely does not include zero, a further indication of the significance of the Pearson correlation coefficient.

The example above illustrates the importance of incorporating known uncertainty in the estimated accuracy for the confidence level category. The relationship between confidence and accuracy should take into account (1)

---

[4]See pages 1310–1311 of Juslin, Olsson, and Winman for the data in their Table 2 and Figure 2, respectively.

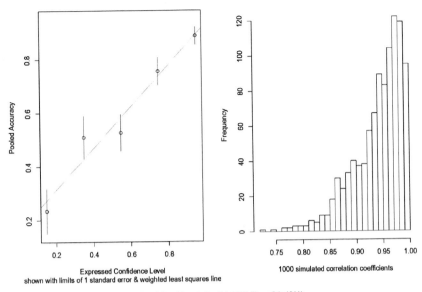

Expressed Confidence Level
shown with limits of 1 standard error & weighted least squares line

1000 simulated correlation coefficients

Data inferred from Juslin et al. 1996, Figure 2 (p.1311)

FIGURE C-1 Data Inferred from Juslin, Olsson, and Winman.
NOTE: Adapted from Juslin, Olsson, and Winman, "Calibration and Diagnosticity of Confidence in Eyewitness Identification." The left panel plots confidence-accuracy data from p. 1311. Data are pooled into five categories; accuracies are inferred from p. 1313. Data are shown with limits of one standard error and weighted least squares regression line. The right panel is a histogram of 1000 simulated Pearson correlation coefficients, using data from 5 categories shown in right panel. The central 90% of the simulated values lie between 0.853 and 0.993, indicating that the true unweighted Pearson correlation coefficient is significantly different from zero. Courtesy of Karen Kafadar.

the repeated responses of a limited number of "eyewitnesses" in the study and (2) the uncertainty in an eyewitness' "expressed confidence level." The 2009 National Research Council report, *Strengthening Forensic Science in the United States: A Path Forward*, cited studies in which fingerprint examiners reached different conclusions when presented with exactly the same evidence at a later time.[5] Quite possibly, in many of these laboratory studies on which these confidence–accuracy relationships are based, participants

---

[5]National Research Council, *Strengthening Forensic Science in the United States: A Path Forward* (Washington, DC: The National Academies Press, 2009), p. 139.

may express different levels of confidence if presented with exactly the same set of circumstances and procedures 6 months later.

The existing literature varies in its assessment of the significance of the confidence–accuracy relationship, with some articles suggesting a very strong relationship and many others suggesting that the relationship is weak or nonexistent. The lack of significance in the confidence–accuracy relationship may result from other factors not taken into account. For example, Smalarz and Wells suggest that restricting the plot to only those data corresponding to "choosers" may strengthen the relationship.[6] Other factors that might affect the relationship include the presence or absence of weapon, the level of stress during the incident, and the length of exposure to the perpetrator. Roediger and colleagues state that

> the simple assumption usually made that confidence and accuracy are always tightly linked is wrong...the relation between confidence and accuracy depends on the method of analysis, on the target material being remembered, on who is doing the remembering, and (in situations where memory is tested by recognition) on the nature of the lures and distractors. In addition, there is more than one way to measure the relationship between confidence and accuracy, and not every way is equally relevant to what courts of law would like to know about the issue.[7]

Studies that incorporate numerous variables, as well as soliciting a confidence statement at various times (e.g., immediately, or 10 minutes after the incident, or 1 hour after the incident), would be valuable.

RECEIVER OPERATING CHARACTERISTIC ANALYSIS

A receiver operator characteristic (ROC) is a reliable, time-honored assessment of test performance. ROC has been used for decades in the medical test diagnostic literature. Conventionally, as noted in Chapter 5, two procedures were compared using a single diagnosticity ratio: $DR = HR/FAR = hit\ rate/false\ alarm\ rate$, or $sensitivity\ /\ (1 - specificity)$. Wixted and colleagues observed that the diagnosticity ratio, DR, can vary depending

---

[6]L. Smalarz and G. L. Wells, "Eyewitness Certainty as a System Variable," in *Reform of Eyewitness Identification Procedures*, ed. B. L. Cutler (Washington, DC: American Psychological Association, 2013), 161–177.

[7]Roediger, Wixted, and DeSoto, "The Curious Complexity Between Confidence and Accuracy in Reports from Memory.

on an eyewitness' ECL and hence proposed the use of an ECL-based ROC curve to compare two lineup procedures (simultaneous versus sequential).[8]

The ECL-based ROC curve for a given procedure (e.g., simultaneous) is constructed as follows:

1) Collect participants in a study and subject them to the experimental conditions.
2) For each participant, record whether she or he accurately selected the correct suspect or accurately passed over the filler and the expressed confidence level in the decision.
3) Collect all the responses for participants who answered "100% confident" (say, n_1 of them) and record the combined *FAR* (false alarm rate, or 1 – specificity) and *HR* (hit rate, or sensitivity) across n_1 participants (FAR_1, HR_1).
4) Repeat step 3 for all participants who answered "90% confident" (or higher; say, $n_{0.9}$ of them), resulting in the data pair ($FAR_{0.9}$, $HR_{0.9}$).
5) Repeat step 3 for all participants who answered "80% confident" (or higher; say, $n_{0.8}$), resulting in the data pair ($FAR_{0.8}$, $HR_{0.8}$).
6) Continue to repeat step 3 for the groups of participants who answered "70% confident" ... "10% confident" (or higher; say, $n_{0.7}$... $n_{0.1}$ of them).
7) Plot the 10 data pairs, (FAR_1, HR_1), ..., ($FAR_{0.1}$, $HR_{0.1}$).

This plot results in the ROC curve, whose points (*HR*, *FAR*) correspond to different ECLs.

The plotted points usually are connected by straight lines, and the slope of the ROC curve at each of those plotted points represents the *DR* corresponding to that confidence category. The ROC curve illustrates the separate *DR*s rather than calculating a single *DR* collapsed across all confidence categories. As with the confidence–accuracy relationship, it is important to recognize the uncertainty in the estimated (*FAR*, *HR*) data points. How does the uncertainty in *FAR* and *HR*, and hence in the diagnosticity ratio (*DR* = *HR/FAR*), translate into uncertainty into the ROC curve?

The effect of uncertainty in estimates of *HR, FAR, DR* (= *HR/FAR*) on the ROC curve can be seen by simulating new *HR* and *FAR* rates,

[8]L. Mickes, H. D. Flowe, and J. T. Wixted, "Receiver Operating Characteristic Analysis of Eyewitness Memory: Comparing the Diagnostic Accuracy of Simultaneous and Sequential Lineups," *Journal of Experimental Psychology: Applied* 18: 361–376 (2012). See especially pp. 362–365 for a description of ROC analysis in the medical literature and applied to the eyewitness identifications.

assuming that the observed HR and FAR rates are true "means" from the simulated distributions. As a first example, consider the set of data from Brewer and Wells[9] which is cited by Mickes, Flowe, and Wixtedin their Table 1.[10] The data are: HR = (.090,.237,.320,.355,.370); FAR = (.002,.015,.030,.038,.041), leading to five diagnosticity ratios (rounded) DR = (45,16,11,9,9). The article states that the experiment involved 1,200 participants.

As above, one can simulate each of the five hit rates and the five false alarm rates, with 4,000 independent trials and 1,200 participants, in such a way that the means of the five distributions of hit rates (HRs) and the means of the five distributions of false alarm rates ($FARs$) equal the values observed in the experiment [e.g., 0.090, 0.237, 0.320, 0.355, 0.370 for HR and (0.002, 0.015, 0.030, 0.038, 0.041) for FAR], leading to five distributions of 4,000 diagnosticity ratios (HR/FAR). For example, consider simulating 1,200 individuals whose HR is 0.090 = 9.0%. One expects that, on average, about (9%) × 1,200 = 108 of the simulated 1,200 participants will have "hits." When repeating this trial of 1,200 individuals, the number might be 110, or 95, or some other number around, but usually not exactly, 108. Repeating the trial 4,000 times, one can average the 4,000 numbers (e.g., 108, 110, 95...) and divide by 1,200, yielding a mean simulated HR. The advantage is that one can also use the 4,000 numbers to calculate a standard deviation.[11] One repeats exactly the same exercise for the five FAR rates, yielding a mean FAR and a standard deviation, SD_{FAR}. As noted in Chapter 5, in real life, HR and FAR will be estimated on the same set of 1,200 participants, so the two numbers, HR and FAR, in the five (HR, FAR) pairs, will be correlated. In the simulation, HR and FAR are independent, so the estimated uncertainties are likely to be optimistic; the real uncertainties could well be larger. One can then plot three sets of points (each set contains five points): (1) (mean HR, mean FAR) (this plot should look qualitatively similar to the one in Figure 6(A) in Mickes, Flowe and Wixted;[12] (2) (mean HR – SD_{HR}, mean FAR – SD_{FAR}) [these points should lie somewhat below the points plotted in (1)[; and (3) (mean HR + SD_{HR}, mean FAR + SD_{FAR}) [these points should lie somewhat above the points plotted in (1)].

---

[9]N. Brewer and G. L. Wells, "The Confidence-Accuracy Relationship in Eyewitness Identification: Effects of Lineup Instructions, Foil Similarity, and Target-Absent Base Rates," *Journal of Experimental Psychology: Applied* 12(1): 11–30 (2012) (as cited by Mickes et al., Table 1, p. 367).

[10]Mickes, Flowe, and Wixted, p. 367.

[11]Or Standard Deviation Hit Rate (SD_{HR}), which also can be obtained from standard formulas for the standard deviation of the binomial distribution. See G. Snedecor and W. Cochran, *Statistical Methods, Sixth Ed.* (Ames, Iowa: Iowa State University Press, 1967).

[12]Mickes, Flowe, and Wixted, p. 371.

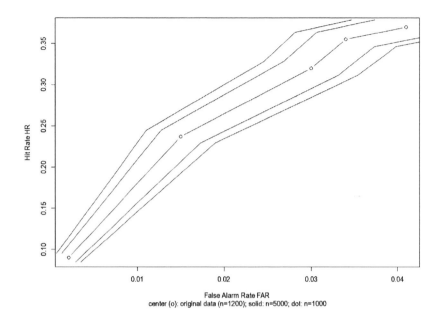

FIGURE C-2 Data from Brewer and Wells.
NOTE: Adapted from Brewer and Wells, "The confidence-accuracy relationship in eyewitness identification." The data are cited by Mickes, Flowe, and Wixted, "Receiver Operating Characteristic Analysis of Eyewitness Memory." Courtesy of Karen Kafadar.

Figure C-2 shows bands of one standard error in both *HR* and *FAR*, illustrating one source of uncertainty in the ROC curve due to estimating *HR* and *FAR*. The same approach to calculating uncertainties was used for the two sets of (*HR, FAR*) values given by the "simultaneous" and "sequential" data in Mickes, Flowe, and Wixted, Table 3.[13] The text indicates that Experiment 1A used *n* = 598 participants, so the simulation assumed *n* = 600. In Figure C-3, "M" refers to "siMultaneous," and "Q" refers to "seQuential." Note that the "M" and "Q" points fall roughly in the same pattern as in Mickes, Flowe, and Wixted's Figure 6A.[14] Note the substantial overlap in the bands of "one standard deviation" surrounding each of the data points, indicating no "statistically significant" differences between the "M" (simultaneous) and "Q" (sequential) points.[15] If one were to take

---

[13]Ibid, p. 372.
[14]Ibid, p. 371.
[15]The bands of two standard deviations would overlap even more.

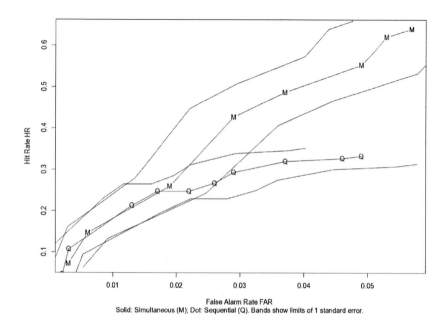

Solid: Simultaneous (M); Dot: Sequential (Q). Bands show limits of 1 standard error.

FIGURE C-3 Data from Experiment 1A in Mickes, Flowe, and Wixted.
NOTE: Adapted from Mickes, Flowe, and Wixted, "Receiver Operating Characteristic Analysis of Eyewitness Memory." Courtesy of Karen Kafadar.

into account the effects of using the *same* eyewitness in the same study with
different responses to different tasks, the variability would be even larger.

When the same exercise is repeated for the data in Experiment 2
(n=631), similarly ambiguous results (see Figure C-4) are obtained. As
Mickes and colleagues suggest, the differences between simultaneous and
sequential are even less impressive, and especially so once bands of one
standard errors around the points are shown.

These further analyses on these published data sets suggest the following conclusions.

1) The strength of the confidence-accuracy relationship involves uncertainty in the measures of both A (accuracy) and C (confidence),
as well as other factors that can influence the relationship.

2) A ROC curve incorporates more information than a single DR
(diagnosticity ratio = HR/FAR) using a third variable [different
test thresholds in the medical literature; in the present context,
different expressed confidence levels (ECLs); i.e., HR and FAR at

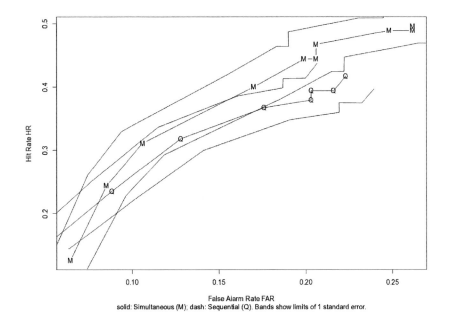

Hit Rate HR

False Alarm Rate FAR
solid: Simultaneous (M); dash: Sequential (Q). Bands show limits of 1 standard error.

FIGURE C-4 Data from Experiment 2 in Mickes, Flowe, and Wixted.
NOTE: Adapted from Mickes, Flowe, and Wixted, "Receiver Operating Characteristic Analysis of Eyewitness Memory." Courtesy of Karen Kafadar.

different expressed confidence levels]. As is true with any data, the data from which a ROC is constructed (*FAR*s, *HR*s, expressed confidence levels) have uncertainty, and that uncertainty is passed on to the ROC. A comparison of two ROCs without recognizing that uncertainty can be misleading. As with any tool, one must be careful in how one draws inferences when comparing ROC curves.

3) Other methods for comparing two procedures (in which the outcome is a binary classification such as "identification" / "no identification" of an individual) exist in other literature.[16]

These analyses considered only the most obvious form of random measurement error. The ROC may be influenced by other sources of bias; these sources are not considered or displayed in the plots shown here (see Chapter 5). Also, the ROC curve takes into consideration only the prob-

---

[16]See, e.g., T. Hastie, R. Tibshirani, and J.H. Friedman, *The Elements of Statistical Learning: Data Mining, Inference, and Prediction* (New York: Springer, 2009) for a discussion on classification and evaluation methods of statistical machine learning research.

ability that an eyewitness who makes a positive identification of a suspect has correctly identified the true culprit (positive predictive value); it does not take into consideration the rule-out probability that an eyewitness who fails to make an identification of a suspect has correctly recognized that the suspect is *not* the true culprit (negative predictive value) (see Chapter 5).

ALTERNATIVE ANALYSIS TO CONFIDENCE-BASED ROC FOR COMPARING PROCEDURES

As noted in Chapter 5, the diagnosticity ratio [hit rate/false alarm rate = HR/FAR = sensitivity/$(1 - \text{specificity})$] can depend not only on an eyewitness' tendency toward "conservative" or "liberal" identification (as measured by expressed confidence level), but also on numerous other factors, including: (1) lineup procedure (e.g., two levels: simultaneous versus sequential); (2) presence or absence of a weapon (two levels; more levels could be considered, such as gun, knife, towel, none); (3) stress (e.g., three levels: high, medium, low); (4) elapsed time between incident and exam (e.g., three levels: 30 min, 2 hours, 1 day); (5) race difference (e.g., two levels: same or different race or four levels: eyewitness/culprit = white/white; white/non-white; non-white/white; non-white/non-white; non-white/white); (6) participant (e.g., N levels, corresponding to N participants).

If a study is sufficiently large, one could develop a performance metric for each participant in the study corresponding to each of these conditions. For example, one could construct a ROC curve and calculate as the performance metric the logarithm of the area under the curve, or $\log(AUC)$, for each person and each condition in the study. One could also use as a performance metric the logarithm of the odds (log odds) of a correct decision; e.g., $\log(HR/(1-HR))$ or $\log((1-FAR)/FAR)$.

Consider the following approach:

Let $y_{ijklmnr}$ denote the $\log(AUC)$ or a log odds (or another performance metric) for the rth trial using participant n ($n = 1, ...,N$) for procedure i, weapon level j, stress level k, time condition l, and cross-race effect m.[17] One could write:

$$y_{ijklmnr} = \mu + \alpha_i + \beta_j + \gamma_k + \delta_l + \phi_m + (\alpha\beta)_{ij} + ...(\textit{interactions})... + \varepsilon_{ijklmnr}$$

---

[17]When the performance metric is a log odds, this model is known as logistic regression; see, e.g., F. Harrell, *Regression Modeling Strategies* (New York: Springer-Verlag, 2001). A model where the performance metric is $\log(AUC)$ was studied by F. Wang and C. Gatsonis. See F. Wang and C. Gatsonis, "Hierarchical Models for ROC Curve Summary Measures: Design and Analysis of Multi-Reader, Multi-Modality Studies of Medical Tests," *Statistics in Medicine* 27: 243-256 (2008).

where μ represents the overall average log(*AUC*) or log odds across all conditions, the next six terms reflect the main effects of A (lineup procedure: $i = 1$ for sequential and $i = 2$ for simultaneous); B (weapon: $j = 1$ for presence and $j = 2$ for absence of weapon); C (stress level: $k = 1$ for low, $k = 2$ for medium, $k = 3$ for high); D (elapsed time between incident and report: $\ell = 1$ for 30 minutes, $\ell = 2$ for 2 hours, $\ell = 3$ for 1 day); E (cross-race effect: $m = 1$ for same race and $m = 2$ for different races); F (participant effect: $n = 1, 2, ...,N$ participants); "*(interactions)*" reflects the joint effect of two or more factors together; and the last term, $\varepsilon_{ijklmnr}$ represents any random error in the rth trial that is not specified from the previous terms (e.g., measurement, "ECL," multiple trials). This approach would allow one to separate the effects of the different factors, to assess which factors have the greatest influence on the outcome (here, logarithm of the area under the ROC curve: bigger is better), and to evaluate the importance of these factors relative to variation among "eyewitnesses." It may be that eyewitnesses are the greatest source of variability, dominating the effects of all other factors. Or it may be that, in spite of person-to-person variability, one or more factors still stand out as having strong influence on the outcome. Note that (1) other covariates could be included, such as age and gender of participant; and (2) the ROC curve need not be defined in terms of expressed confidence level thresholds if a more sensitive measure of response bias (tendency toward "liberal" versus "conservative" identifications) can be developed.

For example, C. A. Carlson and M. A. Carlson[18] use *partial area under the curve*, or *pAUC*, as a summary measure of the information in an ROC curve (bigger is better), for each of twelve different conditions defined by three factors: (1) Procedure, three levels: simultaneous (SIM: suspect in position 4), sequential (SEQ2: suspect in position 2), sequential (SEQ5: suspect in position 5); (2) Weapon focus, two levels: present versus absent; (3) Distinctive feature, two levels: present versus absent. The data are provided in their Table 3, along with 95% confidence intervals.[19] Because the length of a confidence interval is proportional to the standard error, *pAUC* values with shorter confidence intervals correspond to smaller standard errors and hence should have higher weights. The logarithms of the reported *pAUC* values and weights (reciprocals of the lengths of the reported confidence intervals) are given below in Table C-1.

For the Carlson study, the data on all $N = 2,675$ participants (720 undergraduates and 1,955 SurveyMonkey respondents) were combined, and

[18]C. A. Carlson and M. A. Carlson, "An Evaluation of Lineup Presentation, Weapon Presence, and a Distinctive Feature Using ROC Analysis," *Journal of Applied Research in Memory and Cognition* 3(2): 45–53 (2014).
[19]Ibid., p. 49.

TABLE C-1 Conditions and Logarithms of Reported *pAUC* Values[a]

Condition	Procedure	Weapon	Feature	5 + log(*pAUC*)	Weight
1	SIM	Yes	Yes	1.31112	47.6
2	SIM	Yes	No	1.72983	33.3
3	SIM	No	Yes	0.92546	55.6
4	SIM	No	No	1.87643	45.5
5	SEQ2	Yes	Yes	1.49344	47.6
6	SEQ2	Yes	No	1.22774	47.6
7	SEQ2	No	Yes	1.08798	52.6
8	SEQ2	No	No	1.58875	41.7
9	SEQ5	Yes	Yes	1.70316	38.5
10	SEQ5	Yes	No	0.98262	58.8
11	SEQ5	No	Yes	0.65719	66.7
12	SEQ5	No	No	1.49344	55.6

[a]Adapted from data on *pAUC* from Table 3 in C. A. Carlson and M. A. Carlson. "An Evaluation of Lineup Presentation, Weapon Presence, and a Distinctive Feature Using ROC Analysis," *Journal of Applied Research in Memory and Cognition* 3(2): 45–53 (2014). The addition of "5" to log(*pAUC*) is simply to avoid negative numbers; the inferences from the analysis remain unchanged. Courtesy of Karen Kafadar.

expressed confidence levels were solicited on a 7-point scale. Variations in the twelve log($pAUC$) values can be decomposed into three main effects (one each for procedure, weapon, and feature), and their two-way interactions. (The raw data may permit a more detailed analysis.) The data can be analyzed using a less complex model than that stated above (because the model has fewer terms):

$$y_{ijk} = \mu + \alpha_i + \beta_j + \gamma_k + (\alpha\beta)_{ij} + (\alpha\gamma)_{ik} + (\beta\gamma)_{jk} + \varepsilon_{ijk}$$

where y_{ijk} denotes $(5 + \log(pAUC))$ for procedure i ($i = 1, 2, 3$), weapon condition j ($j = 1, 2$), and feature k ($k = 1, 2$); μ represents the overall average log($pAUC$) across all conditions; α_i represents the effect of procedure i; βj represents the effect of weapon condition j; γ_k represents the effect of feature condition k; and the next three terms reflect the three two-factor interactions between the main factors. The analysis of variance, where log($pAUC$) values are weighted according to the values in the last column of Table C-1, is given in Table C-2 below. None of the factors is significant.[20] It must be stressed that the complete set of raw data may yield a more powerful analysis with different results, as might a different summary measure of the ROC curve, such as AUC, or area under the ROC curve.[21]

---

[20]We can decompose the two degrees of freedom in the sum of squares for *Procedure* (three levels), 8.04, into two single degree of freedom contrasts, *SEQ2* versus *SEQ5* (4.14), and *sim* versus the average of *SEQ2* and *SEQ5* (3.90), and consider all pairwise interaction terms among the four "main effects." All single degree-of-freedom effects remain non-significant, in either this weighted analysis or in an unweighted analysis.

[21]For a discussion of the advantages and disadvantages of using AUC versus $pAUC$ as a summary measure, see S. D. Walter, "The Partial Area Under the Summary ROC Curve," *Statistics in Medicine* 24(13): 2025–2040 (July 2005).

TABLE C-2 Analysis of Variance Table for $\log(pAUC)^a$

Source of Variation	Degrees of Freedom	Sum of Squares	Mean Square	F-statistic	p-value
Procedure	2	8.04	4.02	1.129	0.470
Weapon	1	2.94	2.94	0.826	0.460
Feature	1	14.72	14.72	4.138	0.179
Procedure×Weapon	2	0.59	0.30	0.083	0.923
Procedure×Feature	2	10.41	5.21	1.463	0.406
Weapon×Feature	1	34.80	34.80	9.780	0.089
Residuals	2	7.12	3.56		

^{a}Adapted from data on $pAUC$ from Table 3 in C. A. Carlson and M. A. Carlson. "An Evaluation of Lineup Presentation, Weapon Presence, and a Distinctive Feature Using ROC Analysis," *Journal of Applied Research in Memory and Cognition* 3(2): 45–53 (2014). Courtesy of Karen Kafadar.